The Motive

Also by Patrick Lencioni

The Motive

WHY SO MANY LEADERS ABDICATE THEIR
MOST IMPORTANT RESPONSIBILITIES

A LEADERSHIP FABLE

Patrick Lencioni

WILEY

Library of Congress Cataloging-in-Publication Data:

Names: Lencioni, Patrick, 1965- author.
Title: The motive : why so many leaders abdicate their most important
    responsibilities / Patrick Lencioni.
Description: Hoboken, New Jersey : John Wiley & Sons, Inc., [2020] |
    Includes index.
Identifiers: LCCN 2019045547 (print) | LCCN 2019045548 (ebook) | ISBN
    9781119600459 (hardback) | ISBN 9781119600442 (adobe pdf) | ISBN
    9781119600466 (epub)
Subjects: LCSH: Leadership. | Leadership--Moral and ethical aspects.
Classification: LCC HD57.7 .L4489 2020 (print) | LCC HD57.7 (ebook) | DDC
    658.4/092–dc23
LC record available at https://lccn.loc.gov/2019045547
LC ebook record available at https://lccn.loc.gov/2019045548

Printed in the United States of America

F385318_010220

This book is dedicated to Sister Regina Marie Gorman and Weldon Larson, for your precious witness of faith and deep humility as leaders.

CONTENTS

INTRODUCTION

Whenever I hear a graduation speaker exhort a group of students to "go out into the world and be a leader," I want to stand up and shout, "No!!! Please don't be a leader, unless you're doing it for the right reason, and you probably aren't!" Let me explain.

This is the eleventh or twelfth business book I've written, depending on how you count them. If someone were to dive into a stack of my books for the first time, I'd tell them to start with this one.

That's because the majority of the other books I've written focus on *how* to be a leader: How to run a healthy organization, lead a cohesive team, manage a group of employees. However, over the years I've come to the realization that some people won't embrace the instructions I provide because of *why* they wanted to become a leader in the first place.

Throughout my childhood, people exhorted me and my peers to be leaders. I accepted their encouragement at face value and sought opportunities to lead people and organizations from the moment I could captain a team or run for student council. But, like so many people, I never stopped to consider *why* I should be a leader.

As it turns out, the primary motive for most young people, and too many older ones, is the rewards that leadership brings with it. Things like notoriety, status, and power. But people who are motivated by these things won't embrace the demands of leadership when they see little or no connection between doing their duties and receiving those rewards. They'll pick and choose how they spend their time and energy based on what they are going to *get*, rather than what they need to *give* to the people they're supposed to be leading. This is as dangerous as it is common. The purpose of *The Motive* is to make it a little less common.

I hope that this book helps you understand and, perhaps, adjust your leadership motive so that you can fully embrace the difficult and critical nature of leading an organization. Or, perhaps, it will help you come to the peaceful conclusion that you might not want to be a leader at all and allow you to find a better use for your talents and interests in a different role.

The Fable

THE SITUATION

S hay Davis knew that it was too soon for him to get fired. Six months was not enough time for even the most aggressive private equity firm to axe a recently promoted CEO. But it wasn't too soon for them to start thinking about it.

Golden Gate Security wasn't exactly failing under Shay's brief period of leadership. The company, headquartered in Emeryville, a mostly commercial town on the eastern shore of the San Francisco Bay, was still growing, albeit more slowly than most other regional security companies in the west. Profit margins were solid, but they looked anemic compared to those of All-American Alarm, the massive and most aggressive national company in the home and small business security market.

Shay figured that the private equity guys would give him another nine months to jump-start Golden Gate, but he wasn't going to wait that long. After climbing the ladder for more than two decades and finally making it to the top, he wasn't about to let all those years of hard work go to waste.

So he decided to throw his pride out the window and make a painful phone call.

RESEARCH

Lighthouse Partners was a small consulting firm located in Half Moon Bay, California, that had a reputation for working with interesting and successful clients. One of those clients was Del Mar Alarm, a San Diego–based company that was the shining star of the regional security arena in California and a small thorn in Shay Davis's side.

Whether it was a panel discussion at a trade show or an article in a business magazine, Del Mar and its British-born CEO, Liam Alcott, were regularly lauded for their off-the-chart profitability as well as for their ability to fend off national competitors like All-American.

Normally, Shay would never have considered hiring a competitor's consulting firm, but he was beginning to feel desperate enough to try something new. When he contacted the consultant at Lighthouse who worked with Del Mar, she explained that she'd have to check with her client to see if it would be okay for her to work with another company in the same industry. Shay decided he probably wouldn't hear back from her. He was right.

But he could never have predicted what would happen next.

NEMESIS

I t's hard to hate someone you don't know, but Shay figured he was getting pretty good at it in regard to Liam Alcott.

Though he had never really met Alcott, aside from a handshake or a perfunctory greeting at an industry event, Shay had heard him speak a few times and read more print interviews than he cared to remember. He had grown to resent the phony affability of the man who seemed to have such an easy time doing what Shay hadn't yet figured out.

So when Shay's assistant, Rita, came into his office to announce that someone named Liam was calling for him on line one, Shay figured it was one of his own executives pulling a prank on him. But before he could pick up the phone to play along, he noticed the 619 area code and decided that the caller might just be his nemesis from San Diego.

Taking a deep breath, he dove in. "This is Shay."

"Hello, Shay. This is Liam Alcott."

Shay realized immediately that it wasn't a prank. But he was somehow relieved that he didn't even like the sound of the man's voice, notwithstanding the English accent, which he decided was affected. So he decided to be excessively nice.

"Well, what can I do for you, Liam?"

"First, I want to apologize for not reaching out to you last summer to congratulate you on your promotion. I feel like a bum."

Shay wasn't at all convinced that the man was genuine. But he wasn't about to let on. "Don't be silly. Believe me, if anyone knows how busy you are, it's me."

"I suppose that's true. Anyway, I'm calling because Amy over at Lighthouse told me that you contacted her about working with them."

Shay felt a rush of shame wash over him, expecting Liam to chastise him for trying to poach his consultants, not to mention his intellectual property. Shay tried to play it cool. "Yeah. I just figured that they know our industry, and that if they didn't have a problem with—"

Liam interrupted. "Of course. I get it. And I don't have any problem with it at all. Amy's a great consultant, and Lighthouse has been very helpful to us down here. You would love working with her."

More than a little surprised, Shay backed off to preserve some pride. "Well, we're going to be talking to other firms too, so we're not ready to commit to anything quite yet."

Liam didn't flinch. "That's smart. In fact, before you hire any consultants, I think there is one big thing that you should do first."

Shay was bracing himself for some sort of condescending advice. "What's that?"

"You should let me tell you what we've learned from Lighthouse and see if that might be enough for you."

Shay didn't know how to respond. *Did I hear that correctly?*

Before he could think of something to say, Liam continued. "In fact, I'm coming up there next Thursday for a meeting, and then I'm staying the weekend at my sister-in-law's in Walnut Creek. Why don't we get together on Friday?"

"I'll have to check with—"

"I just asked your assistant, Rita. It's Rita, right?"

"Yeah."

"She said you're wide open Friday. You were sup-posed to do an ops review or something but it got pushed back a few weeks."

Shay suddenly felt betrayed—by Rita, by the con-sultants at Lighthouse, by someone. Not ready to accept his enemy's clearly devious offer, he pushed back.

"Don't take this wrong, Liam," he paused, "but don't you have some reservations about sharing your secrets with a competitor?"

Liam laughed. "Competitor? I don't think we're competitors. I mean, I certainly wouldn't have wanted Lighthouse to work with you if we were. And it's not like we're trying to steal one another's customers, unless you have plans to get into the security business in San Diego. So I don't see us having any conflict here."

Shay tried desperately to think of an excuse.

Liam continued. "I'd say that our common enemy is All-American, and I'd rather not see them get another regional foothold in Northern California." He paused.

"Unless you've already figured out how to deal with them."

Though Shay didn't like the idea of admitting any weakness, he also didn't want to lose out on any advice that Liam might have for him. "No, we've still got work to do there."

"Okay," Liam announced enthusiastically, "so that's one area where I might be able to help you. And I'm sure you'll have some advice for me."

Shay responded with a partially false show of humility. "Well, I don't know about that." Deciding that he could think of no good reason to refuse Liam's offer, he relented. "All right then. What time should we meet on Friday?"

When the call ended, Shay decided he'd have a few days to come up with a good reason to be out of town at the end of next week.

DEFENSELESS

B y the close of the day, Shay realized he was stuck. It wasn't that he lacked the cleverness to come up with a believable excuse. He had plenty of small business customers he could schedule a meeting with on a moment's notice. That wasn't the problem. Shay's predicament was having to choose between two threats to his pride.

On the one hand, canceling the meeting would allow him to avoid the humiliation of a lecture from a man he disliked. On the other hand, missing out on good advice from a more successful company might cause him to forfeit more market share to All-American Alarm, which would embarrass him in front of his board and possibly lead to his eventual demise. Deciding that losing his job would be worse than admitting his inferiority to Liam, Shay decided to go ahead and meet with his adversary to learn what he could about how to deal with their mutual competitor.

But when he woke up on Friday, he lay in bed staring at the ceiling, wondering if he had made the right decision.

Turning to his wife, Dani, who had just woken up, Shay asked her a strange question. "Isn't there some really important chore you need me to do right away so I don't have to go to work?"

Dani laughed. "You must have a lot of meetings today."

"I wish." Shay responded, wondering if he should confess his pettiness to his wife.

"What's the problem then?"

"Oh, I'm just being stupid. I have to spend a lot of time with someone I don't particularly enjoy."

"Brandon?" she asked.

"No."

"Marisa?"

Shay climbed out of bed. "No, it's no one from the company."

Dani seemed puzzled. "Who is it?"

"Oh, I don't know," he answered as he disappeared into the bathroom.

"What do you mean 'you don't know'? Who is it?"

"It's a guy named Liam Alcott."

"You mean that CEO from San Diego who you hate so much?" Dani shouted so her husband could hear her from the other room.

Shay came back into the bedroom. "Have I complained about him that much?"

"Are you kidding? *'Liam Alcott is a pompous ass. Liam Alcott thinks he's God's gift to business. Liam Alcott's accent is so fake that*—'"

Shay interrupted his wife. "Okay, I get it. I guess I have."

Dani got up and started making the bed. "So why are you meeting with him?"

"I don't know. It's weird. He offered to help me with something."

"Did he offer to help you make the bed?"

"What?" Shay was confused.

She pointed to his side of the bed.

"Oh. Sorry." He started to pull up the sheets and blanket.

"So what's this meeting about?" she persisted.

Shay didn't want to tell her the whole story. "He wants to help figure out how to compete better with All-American."

"That's a good thing, right?"

"If it were anyone else ..." He didn't finish the sentence.

"Well, I'd say you need to take a breath, put your big boy pants on, and admit that he might know something you don't." She paused while he took her advice. "And if he's a pompous ass, thank him for his time and be the bigger person."

"You know," Shay stopped making the bed for a moment. "I don't remember asking for your opinion." He smiled.

Dani threw a pillow at him and responded with a British accent. "I'm sorry. Was I being a pompous ass?"

INVASION

When Shay walked into his office, he found Liam sitting behind his desk with his feet propped up on it, smoking a cigar.

"So, big boy. Let me tell you how to run a business."

No, that's not true. But Liam was already sitting in the lobby of the building waiting for him.

"Good morning, Shay!" Liam announced as he stood up, with more enthusiasm than Shay would have liked this early in the morning.

Still, he mustered up the energy to respond in kind. "It's nice to finally meet you, Liam. Thanks so much for doing this."

"Hey, it's a chance to avoid having to spend too much time with my in-laws."

Shay laughed inauthentically, like one of those characters in a bad sitcom.

The two continued their small talk as they made their way toward Shay's office, stopping by the kitchen to get coffee.

Arriving at the CEO's well-appointed office with a view of Alcatraz, they sat down at a couch, and Shay began.

"So, where should we start?"

Liam was ready with an answer. "Well, why don't you tell me why you called Lighthouse? What were you hoping to get from them?"

Shay felt a sudden rush of shame again, wondering if this wasn't an accusation. Liam seemed to read his mind.

"Oh, I'm not questioning your intentions, Shay. Not at all." He held up his hands in a show of apology. "I'm just wondering what you were feeling that made you look for help."

Relieved by the reassurance, Shay wondered if Liam might be a little less pompous than he had assumed. He decided he could open up a little.

"Well, I'm feeling like we're just not firing on all cylinders here." *Okay, that wasn't so bad,* Shay decided.

Liam jotted a word or two in the notebook that he brought with him, and then responded. "Is it mostly about All-American?"

Without thinking, Shay admitted, "Well, that's certainly part of it. But I think there's something else. I just don't know what."

Liam looked up with a big smile on his face and said something that seemed to Shay to be either arrogance or goofiness. "Oooh, this is going to be fun."

At that moment Shay decided he'd made a big mistake.

SURRENDER

Liam noticed that the look on Shay's face had changed, and he seemed concerned. "Oh, I hope I didn't insult you."

"No, not at all." Shay lied.

"My wife says when I get excited I can come across like a dork, and a condescending one at that, especially with my accent." He laughed and explained himself. "It's just that I love this management stuff, but I rarely get a chance to hang out with other CEOs. And I wasn't sure if you'd feel comfortable being so candid."

"Neither did I," Shay announced, a little sarcastically.

They laughed. Shay felt like he was losing control of the conversation, even as he was finding it hard to hate Liam.

"So then, what do your numbers look like?" Liam asked.

Shay seemed a little shocked by the direct request for actual information.

Noticing his new friend's reticence, Liam assured him. "If you want me to sign a nondisclosure, I'd be glad to."

Shay shook his head, waved his hand, and made one of those facial expressions that said *don't be silly.*

"Good," Liam announced. "Because if we're going to help each other, we have to be pretty naked here."

For the next half hour or so, Liam presented the high-level fundamentals of his financial operations, while Shay countered with mostly general answers and a few real numbers sprinkled in here and there for effect.

In some aspects of their businesses, the two companies were quite similar. But in many others, Del Mar was light-years ahead. Shay did his best to hide his surprise at the discrepancy between the companies' results, which he hoped Liam hadn't noticed.

Unfortunately, he did. With a genuinely concerned look on his face, Liam offered, "What's going on up here, my friend?"

Though calm, inside Shay was desperately searching for a believable excuse for his inferiority. "Well, the market is a little different in the Bay Area than it is down south."

Liam didn't seem convinced, so Shay explained.

"Salaries are higher. Local taxes are higher. Cost of living."

Liam listened and nodded with as much empathy as he could muster. Wincing just slightly, he took a breath and finally responded. "Please don't take this wrong, Shay. But those things would only account for a small part of the differences between our companies' performance."

Shay's face indicated neither frustration nor agreement. Nothing.

Liam went on carefully. "I mean, unless I'm hearing things wrong, you seem to have more employees generating less revenue. Your turnover, among both customers and employees, is considerably higher than ours. And you're actually spending more money on marketing than we are." He paused. "Am I missing something?"

Shay shrugged. "Well, at least our company isn't run by a pretentious asshole."

Of course, he didn't say that, but he wanted to, even if he knew it wasn't really fair.

"I'm not going to lie to you," Shay confessed. "This isn't easy for me to hear."

The two CEOs sat in awkward silence for a long five seconds.

Finally, Shay summoned enough courage to ask the question. "So, do you think there is something fundamentally ..." he paused, searching for an acceptable word, "*broken* here? If so, I'd like to know what it is."

Liam shrugged. "I don't know, but I'll be more than happy to help you figure it out."

Shay didn't know what to say, so Liam continued. "Why don't I start by telling you what I learned from Amy and the other consultants at Lighthouse?"

Shay took a deep breath, and thought to himself, *big boy pants.*

NAKED

Liam went to the whiteboard in Shay's office, picked up a black pen, and announced, "Everything that Amy and the other consultants at Lighthouse focused on started with me."

He wrote *CEO* in big letters on the board.

He turned toward Shay like a college professor. "But they redefined the acronym, changing it from chief *executive* officer to chief *executing* officer." He wrote the new term next to the three letters.

Liam didn't see Shay roll his eyes behind his back, but he didn't need to.

"I know what you're thinking," Liam explained. "It sounds cheesy. Big deal. They changed a word."

Shay seemed relieved that Liam shared his cynicism.

"But then I learned that it's actually an important change if you think about it from a grammatical standpoint." He turned back to the words on the board. 'Executive' is a noun. 'Executing' is a verb."

"Technically, it's a participle," Shay explained, a little sheepishly. "I was an English major."

"Well la-dee-da," Liam teased him. "I grew up in England and I'll be damned if I'm going to have a bloody American lecture me about my language."

They laughed, sincerely this time.

Liam continued. "The point is, it conveys activity. The leader is involved in executing rather than simply being an executive."

"The way you used it there, that's a gerund." Shay declared.

"Whatever." Liam laughed.

"But I really hope there's more to this than just the word," Shay complained.

Liam was suddenly surprised, in a good kind of way. "That's exactly what I told them!"

Liam sat back down and continued. "Here's how they explained it to me. See, if you took a survey of a hundred CEOs and asked them what their most important day-to-day activities are, the things they actually do, you'd get about thirty-five substantially different answers."

Shay shrugged. "Well, everyone has different skills and interests. So that makes sense, right?"

Liam responded abruptly. "No. It makes no sense at all."

Shay frowned just slightly at what felt like a rebuke.

"Well," Liam clarified, "I suppose it makes sense that CEOs do it. But it makes no sense in terms of what their companies *need*."

"I'm not sure I agree, but keep going."

"Okay. Let's start with you. What is the most important part of what you do?"

Shay didn't answer, thinking that Liam's question was a rhetorical one.

"I'm actually asking you."

"Oh, sorry." Shay rallied. "I don't know. I do so many things, it's hard to say. I could have Rita go through my calendar, I suppose."

Liam nodded patiently. "I'm not actually asking you for a quantitative breakdown of your time. I'm more curious about what you think you really do to help the business. How do you see your job, in terms of verbs or participles or whatever you want to call them?"

Shay took a breath. "Okay. Let's see." He thought about it for a moment. "I'd say that reviewing our numbers with finance and working with sales and marketing on go-to-market activities would be my most important activities."

Liam went to the whiteboard and recorded those answers while Shay explained.

"I was the head of marketing for four years before becoming CEO, so that's a pretty important part of my job. And it's critical in our industry, as you know. All-American Alarm spends five times what we do on advertising, so we have to be smarter than they are."

"Okay," Liam nodded. "What else?"

Shay looked out the window as though he might find the answer in the San Francisco Bay. "I think that dealing with my board is pretty important. If I don't keep the private equity guys happy, things can get pretty sideways around here."

"All right." He added that to the whiteboard.

Shay finished. "And then there's all the stuff I have to do keep the machine running, I guess. Management. Dealing with employee issues and politics."

Liam captured that as well.

"I'd say those are the most important things." Shay had a sudden realization. "Oh, and I meet with our small business and multiunit housing customers. That's an extremely profitable market, and I need to make sure we're growing in that area."

And that was the final entry on the board, which now displayed the following list:

> Reviewing ops and
> financials
>
> Driving marketing and
> sales programs
>
> Handling the board
>
> Managing and leading
>
> Interacting with
> key customers

"Now I have two more questions," Liam announced. "And they're important ones."

Shay shifted in his chair as though he were preparing himself. He had to admit that he was almost enjoying this.

"First, rank these five activities in terms of which you like to do the most. One is highest. Five is lowest. Then, rank them in terms of their importance." Liam wrote "Enjoyment" in one column and "Importance" in another and handed Shay the black pen.

"Don't you want to know how much of my time I spend in these areas?"

"Nope. We can talk about that later, if we have to. Let's focus on enjoyment and importance first."

Shay went to the board, feeling a little like a fifth-grade student trying to solve a math problem. After a minute or so, he was finished.

	Enjoyment	Importance
Reviewing ops and financials	5	3
Driving marketing and sales programs	1	2
Handling the board	3	5
Managing and leading	4	4
Interacting with key customers	2	1

Shay sat down, and he and Liam studied the information on the whiteboard.

Finally, Shay asked a question. "What are you thinking?"

Before Liam could answer, Shay asked another question. "Is this what your list looks like?"

Liam looked at the board again and answered plainly. "No."

Shay frowned, apparently confused, so Liam explained. "My list would include only one of your items. But that's not the point of this."

Shay seemed to be reexamining the list in light of Liam's comment, trying to guess what he meant.

Liam continued. "But as far as what I enjoy, I'd say our numbers would be very similar …:"

Shay was relieved.

". . . three or four years ago. But today they are very different. And I'm guessing that's part of the problem here."

Shay winced and considered how he might be able to end the conversation early. Fortunately for him, his curiosity was greater than his fear of insult or failure. But just barely.

REVEAL

S hay decided to be as direct as possible. "Okay, what does your list look like?"

Liam went to the board. He drew a line through all of the entries other than managing and leading.

	Enjoyment	Importance
~~Reviewing ops and financials~~	5	3
~~Driving marketing and sales programs~~	1	2
~~Handling the board~~	3	5
Managing and leading	4	4
~~Interacting with key customers~~	2	1

"Oh, come on! Shay reacted. "You're telling me that you don't do any sales or marketing or finance?"

Liam stared at the board while he considered the question, as though the answer were written there. "Well, if you're asking whether I talk about those things with my team, the answer is 'yes'. Of course I do."

He turned and looked at Shay again.

"But the only time I get directly involved in those activities outside of our meetings is when one of my executives is struggling and needs some help or counsel." Liam declared.

Shay pounced. "Okay, you can call it help or counsel or whatever you want, but you still dive in and do sales and finance stuff, right?"

"I don't think we're talking about the same thing."

Shay looked at Liam, studying him carefully as though he were trying to decide on a strategy for exposing his false claim. Finally, he began. "So you're saying you don't drive marketing programs except when there is a problem or when your marketing guy or gal ..."

Liam interrupted. "Gal."

"When your marketing gal is struggling or needs your help."

Liam nodded. "That's right."

Shay wasn't convinced, but he didn't comment right away. Finally, he explained himself. "I'm involved in marketing all the time, probably because I know more about that part of the business than any of my people. I used to run marketing."

Liam nodded, without apparent judgment. "Okay, and what about finances?"

"Well, I probably check in with my CFO every day. I like to know what business has closed, what revenue we've collected, what our cash flow looks like, stuff like that." Feeling like he was being judged, he defended himself. "I think my board expects me to know what's going on with their money."

Again, Liam nodded dispassionately. "Okay."

Shay looked at the categories on the whiteboard and decided to turn the tables on his self-appointed mentor. "So, you don't spend time managing your board?"

Liam shook his head. "Not really. I mean, I meet with them once a quarter, and I take their calls if they need to talk to me, which is pretty rare. And that's about it."

Shay was starting to lose a bit of his courtesy. "I have a hard time believing that."

Liam didn't back off. "I'm sure you do. But it's true. I told my board when I took over that their input, outside of a major catastrophe, would be limited to our quarterly meetings. It was one of my conditions for taking the job. They didn't like it much at first, but now I think they're relieved." There was not a hint of bragging in Liam's response.

Shay shifted his approach. "Don't take this wrong, Liam, because I really appreciate you coming up here and everything. But I can't just sit here and accept all this without a little skepticism."

Liam smiled kindly. "You'd be a fool if you *weren't* skeptical. That's the only way you'll eventually buy in."

Shay toned down his defensiveness a little and attempted to summarize his general sense of disbelief. "Okay. So, you're telling me that you spend almost all of your time leading and managing your team?"

Liam thought about it as if he wanted to be certain. "Yep," he said, nodding emphatically.

Shay smiled. He seemed to be fighting off a mix of incredulity and condescension. Liam didn't seem to mind at all.

"Maybe we just have different ways of doing things," Shay conceded.

"Maybe," Liam answered, unconvinced. "But you're going to have to convince me that your way is working for your company. Are you willing to let me challenge you about that?"

"Of course," Shay said without much enthusiasm. "But before we do that, can we take a fifteen-minute break, so I can make a phone call?"

"Sure," Liam smiled. "But first point me in the direction of the kitchen and the bathroom. Not in that order."

WHERE WERE WE?

When Liam returned almost fifteen minutes later, Shay was just ending his call.

Liam noticed that he had taken a full page of notes during the call and that he made a point of putting them away into one of his desk drawers before grabbing a new notepad and returning to the couch.

"Now, where were we?"

"I was going to ask you some questions about how you do your job." Liam reminded him, just a little disappointed that Shay hadn't remembered.

"Right. Let me have it."

Liam noticed that something had changed in Shay. He was somehow happier, more confident than he had been just fifteen minutes earlier. He dismissed it and pushed on.

"Okay, let's dive into the leadership and management stuff that you think I spend too much of my time doing. Tell me about your meetings."

"What about them?" Shay wasn't the least bit defensive now.

"Are they effective? Do you enjoy them? What is your role? Tell me anything about them."

Shay shrugged. "Well, I definitely don't enjoy them. I mean, who loves meetings?"

With no sign of judgment, Liam continued. "What about them do you dislike the most?"

"Where do I start? They're too long. They're frustrating. They're usually boring. Anything else?"

"Okay, prepare yourself for what I'm about to say." Liam paused for effect. "I actually love meetings."

Shay rolled his eyes. "Come on, man."

They laughed.

"I'm completely serious," Liam confessed. "It's without a doubt my favorite part of my job."

He gave Shay a moment to roll his eyes again before continuing. "But my enjoyment of them isn't the point. The fact is, leading my meetings is one of the most important things I do."

This time Shay didn't laugh or roll his eyes. He just frowned as though he were trying to decide whether to dismiss Liam as a lunatic or give him a chance to explain.

He chose a third option.

"Listen, Liam. My philosophy on meetings is that I go to as few as I can. Yeah, I can't skip them all. Some are pretty important. But most of them suck, and I can't afford to be wasting my time."

Liam didn't jump in right away, and that's when Shay said one of the most telling things of all. "Besides, I've spent half my life going to meetings because I had to. I'll be damned if I'm going to keep doing that now that I don't have to."

Liam wrote something in his notebook and continued. "Okay, let's change the subject," he said without even a hint of judgment. "We can come back to that later."

The look on Shay's face made it clear that he felt he had won that round and that Liam was backing off. He wasn't.

DEEPER

iam changed the subject. "Let's talk about management."

"Before we do that," Shay countered, "can we get out of my office for a while? I'm getting a little claustrophobic." Without waiting for a reply, he continued. "Come on. I'll give you a quick tour, and then we can find another place to talk."

Liam agreed, and they stood and made their way to the door.

For the next fifteen minutes, the two CEOs walked the halls of Golden Gate Security, even stopping by the response center, where Shay's people interacted with law enforcement.

Though the building was certainly professional and stylish, Liam found the atmosphere to be largely stale. Most people worked alone at their desks, with little noise or casual interaction between employees.

Shay introduced Liam to a few of his direct reports, all of whom were quite pleasant, even if none seemed particularly excited to see their boss. Shay seemed especially eager for Liam to meet the company's CFO, who was their final stop on the tour.

Jackie Loureiro, a sharply dressed financial wizard and Shay's most experienced executive, was one of the few people he trusted to work directly with the private equity group who funded their enterprise.

It was clear that Jackie either recognized Liam or knew that he was visiting, because after shaking hands, she wondered out loud, "So what brings our biggest rival up to the Bay Area for a visit?"

Liam smiled. "Do you consider us rivals? I don't think we're rivals, unless someone isn't telling me about your market push in Southern California."

"I didn't say we were competitors," Jackie responded confidently. "A rival is different than a competitor."

Shay jumped in. "I'd say that we're potential partners."

Jackie laughed in a way that suggested Shay had made an inside joke. Liam dismissed it all.

"Anyway, Liam was just about to ask me about how I manage," Shay announced. "I thought you might have some insight on that."

Jackie replied, "*Hands off until the shit hits the fan* is how I'd describe it." She looked at Shay, smiling.

Liam noticed that Shay was less than pleased at the way he was characterized.

Wanting to reduce the awkwardness of the moment, he asked the CFO a quick question. "Is Shay more of a one-on-one kind of manager or a team guy?"

"Both," Jackie responded, almost humorously. "He likes to get us all in a room for staff meetings, but then he goes around the table getting reports from each of us on what we're doing in our respective areas. I find it a little tedious, but that's probably because I see everything through a financial lens."

"So, do you think you're the only one who finds it tedious?" Liam asked.

Shay interrupted before Jackie could answer. "Hell, I find it tedious!"

They laughed.

Shay continued, "I'm guessing everyone else does, too."

Jackie agreed. "It's not that we don't understand the importance of it all. It's just not our favorite way to spend two hours."

"How often do you have staff meetings?" Liam wanted to know.

"Every week," Shay explained. "Monday morning. Nine to eleven. Rain or shine."

"Unless we're traveling or with a customer or doing something critical," Jackie corrected her boss. "Then we can get out of it. It's one of the best incentives for scheduling an analyst meeting on Mondays." She laughed, but not as though she hadn't been serious about her comment.

Shay tried to redirect the conversation. "Like I said before, I prefer real work to meetings, so we try to minimize the time we spend in them."

Jackie agreed. "I'd say we're pretty bottom-line driven around here. If you can't justify what you're doing in terms of how it impacts revenue or customers, you're doing something wrong." She looked over at her computer. "In fact, I've got to return a call from one of our PE guys, so I better get back to work."

Liam and Shay thanked Jackie for her time and left her office.

PUSHING

For some reason, Shay wanted to continue the meeting with Liam outside of the office, so he took him to a very early lunch at Maria's, a Mexican restaurant in a nearby town called San Pablo. They were the only customers in the place.

Before the chips and salsa arrived, Liam resumed his questioning.

"How would you say that Jackie compares to your other execs?"

Shay paused, a little surprised by the question. "Well, she certainly knows what she's doing. I don't have a more competent person on my team."

"How about interpersonal skills and attitude?"

Suddenly Shay seemed to understand what Liam was getting at. "Oh, Jackie's rough around the edges, if that's what you're asking."

"How so?"

"Well, she can definitely rub people the wrong way. She drives half of my team crazy."

"Really?"

"Oh yeah. She's blunt. She doesn't trust them with financial decisions. She's always questioning them about their budgets." Shay seemed to be neither pleased nor troubled by what he was saying.

"How do you feel about that?"

"I don't know" Shay shrugged. "I mean, I wish she were a lot more diplomatic. And I'm tired of hearing people complain about her."

"So have you talked to her about it?" Liam did his best to avoid being judgmental or condescending.

Shay took a deep breath. "Yeah, I've mentioned it to her. She knows."

"She knows how it affects the other executives?"

"Yeah," Shay responded without confidence. "It's pretty obvious, right?"

"I'm guessing it's not all that obvious to her."

Shay frowned, thinking about how to respond. "Here's the deal, Liam. All of my people have their issues. Jackie's too blunt. Karl won't push back on anyone. Margaret never thinks she's wrong. Everybody has something."

"Yeah, that's the same for my people. None of them are perfect."

Shay was glad to have Liam agree with him about something.

Then Liam finished his thought. "And it's my job to help them get better."

Suddenly the look on Shay's face, even his posture, changed. Liam thought he was going to respond in a less than diplomatic way. And then the waitress arrived.

By the time she had taken their orders and disappeared, Shay had lost whatever edge he'd been sharpening earlier. Still, he was less than enthusiastic about what Liam had said.

"Listen, Liam. I hire adults. These people don't need me to babysit them. Most of them have more than a decade of management under their belts. That's one of the reasons I chose them. If I have to coach them all the time and get them to change the way they behave, then I shouldn't have hired them in the first place."

Liam frowned. "Well?"

"Well what?"

"Did you hire the wrong people?"

"What do you mean?"

"I mean you said that Jackie and Karl and Mary—"

Shay corrected him, "Margaret."

"Right, Margaret. You said they have issues. Why haven't you fired them?"

"I didn't say they were horrible. I said they have issues. They're generally competent."

"So their issues don't impact their performance?"

Shay was getting a little frustrated now. "No. I don't know. Everyone has issues."

The waitress arrived with water, chips, and salsa, which gave Liam a moment to think about what to say next.

"Shay, before we go on, let me remind you why I came up here. It wasn't to give you the third degree. It was to help you understand what I learned from Lighthouse. But if I'm being too tough on you—"

Shay interrupted, reassuringly. "No. You're not. I'm sorry. I need this, and I appreciate it. Keep going."

"Okay. Good." Liam responded with relief.

Shay felt the need to explain himself. "It's just that I have so much on my plate. And it feels like I have a lot of better things to do than make Karl learn to stand up for himself."

"Well, if you don't think it affects his performance, then you probably don't need to." Liam couldn't completely hide his patronizing tone.

"I didn't say it didn't affect his performance. It's just that I can't afford to spend all of my time babysitting."

Liam took a deep breath. "Okay, Shay. I'm going to be very direct here. Remember, you just said you need this."

Shay didn't say anything, but didn't seem to be objecting.

Liam went on. "It's not babysitting. It's management. And it's your job."

Had Liam not warned him prior to the comment, Shay might have come unglued. As it was, he calmly fired back. "Maybe we just have different styles. Maybe you find it natural or easy, or maybe you actually enjoy coaching people and staying out of the details of the business. But—"

Liam interrupted him, a mix of shock and frustration on his face. "Easy? Natural? Are you kidding?"

Stunned by the sudden change in temperament, Shay didn't respond.

"You probably don't know about my background." It was a question in the form of a statement.

Shay shook his head.

Liam smiled. "Well, this is about to get interesting."

STREET CREDIBILITY

Liam took a big drink of water and began.

"Well, Shay, I have good news and bad news." He didn't wait for Shay to choose which to start with. "The good news is that you're not going to feel like I'm condescending to you after you hear my story." He paused. "The bad news is you're not going to be able to convince me that this is all just a matter of style difference."

"Okay," Shay said, unsure about what was to come next.

"Nine years ago, I became CEO of a company in London. It was a successful provider of home technology services for residences in the central and southern part of England. We did everything from home video and audio to wireless technology and even some security."

He paused to check in with Shay. "You're sure you haven't heard any of this before?"

His mouth full of chips, Shay shook his head.

Liam continued. "Okay, the market was growing extremely fast. Think about what was happening a decade ago in this space. We were exploding. When I took over, we were a twelve-million-dollar company that had been a three-million-dollar enterprise a year earlier."

"Wow," Shay acknowledged, having swallowed his food.

"Damus, that's what we were called. Damus is the word for 'house' in Latin. Anyway, we were the first big mover in the industry, and we had better technology and brand recognition and talent than any of our competitors. The next biggest company, Bamboo Solutions, was less than a third of our size and was behind us in every way possible. There was only one area where they were better than us."

Having grabbed Shay's attention, Liam decided to pause to increase the impact of what he was about to say. He dipped a chip in the salsa and waited until he had swallowed before announcing, "They had a much better CEO than we did."

Shay seemed surprised by Liam's admission.

"That's right," Liam explained. "Brandon Quinn. Irish guy. Not nearly as smart as I was. Younger. Not much experience, especially in our industry. In terms of salesmanship, finance, technology, strategy, he couldn't hold a candle to me. And I'm not being arrogant here. This poor guy had nothing on me. I actually felt bad for him."

"What happened?"

"Well, to make a long story short—which, according to my wife, I'm not particularly good at—within two and a half friggin' years, Brandon Quinn and Bamboo had stolen half of our customers, a third of our best technicians. Before I knew what had happened, I was fired."

Suddenly Shay was curious. "How did he do that?"

"Well, I didn't know it at the time, but four years ago when I hired Lighthouse, I finally figured it out."

"And?"

Liam took a deep breath. "And that, my friend, is what I came up here to teach you."

BRASS TACKS

"Okay. Tell me," Shay demanded, a little impatiently.

"Well, if you roll your eyes at me one more time, I'm going to pour this salsa over your head."

Shay laughed.

Liam didn't. "I'm serious," he said, then smiled as he corrected himself. "Well, not about the salsa. But I'm getting a little tired of your cynicism. I'm trying to help you here, man."

Shay nodded, surprised to hear such a direct complaint from the formerly affable Englishman. "I get it," Shay acknowledged, "but I still don't quite understand why you're doing this for me. What's in it for you?"

Liam smiled. "Listen, when you go through what I went through and see the damage it does to others, you wouldn't wish that on anyone else."

Shay nodded, partially sold.

Liam continued. "And like I said before, we aren't competitors. If I can help you put a dent in All-American, that's good for both of us."

Shay seemed to gloss over that. "Okay. So what did you learn from Lighthouse?"

Liam took a drink of water. "I learned that I am supposed to have the most painful job in the company."

Shay was thoroughly confused.

Before Liam could explain, the waitress arrived with their food, warning them that the plates were hot. Shay was so immersed in what Liam was saying that he wasn't paying attention and promptly reached out and moved his plate after it had been set down.

"Yow! That's hot!"

The waitress tried to explain to him that she had warned him.

Liam assured her, "It's okay. We weren't paying attention. It's fine."

Still a little embarrassed, she dismissed herself from the table.

Shay recovered quickly. "So, you just said that you're supposed to have the worst job in the company."

Liam corrected him. "The most painful job."

"Whatever," Shay said. "A few minutes ago, you were saying how much you loved meetings and everything."

"I learned to love it," Liam barely managed to communicate audibly with a mouth full of enchilada.

"Okay," Shay asked patronizingly, "you need to explain."

After a few seconds of silence, Liam swallowed and went on. "Look, I love my job. But I wouldn't have loved it three years ago. In fact, I did everything I could to avoid doing it." He paused and took a drink of water. "Like you do."

Shay wanted to defend himself, but didn't know enough about what Liam meant.

"Go on," he said, taking another bite of food.

Liam continued. "Well, I'm a technology guy at heart. That's what I grew up doing, and that's what I'm comfortable with. That's what I spent my time doing before I got fired in England. And don't get me wrong; if I could, I'd still spend my time doing that. But I can't, and I don't."

"Why not?"

"Because I have a CIO and a CTO who focus on those things. I have to be the CEO."

Shay shook his head. "It's not that cut and dried. I mean, yeah you have to be the CEO. But you can still keep your hand in technology stuff. I'm guessing you might be better than the people you hired in those areas anyway."

Liam shrugged. "Maybe. Maybe not. But that's not the point. The point is, I can delegate finance and marketing and sales and technology and operations and all those things. I can't delegate *my job*."

"Who said anything about delegating it? How much of your time does it take to do the CEO stuff?"

"All of it. And then some."

Shay put down his fork. "You mean to tell me that managing your team and the company doesn't give you *any* time to get involved in other parts of the business?"

Liam nodded his head. "That's right."

Shay laughed. "Maybe I should be giving you advice, Liam. I mean, what the hell are you spending all your time doing?"

"And finally, we get to the reason for my visit," Liam smiled bitterly. "And the reason that Del Mar Alarm is kicking your ass."

Shay laughed. "Okay, that's a little cocky, isn't it?"

"Hey, you're pretty confident that you've figured out how to be a CEO," Liam pushed back. "Remember, I didn't call *your* consulting firm looking for advice."

Taking a drink of his water to calm himself down, Shay looked around at the empty restaurant. Struggling to come up with a less-than-harsh response, he thought of his wife. Finally, he said something that even he thought seemed completely out of character, "You're right. I shouldn't be so flippant. You've come up here to help, and I'm not being very open."

Liam held up his hand in apology. "No, I shouldn't have said what I said. I was being flippant. It's just—"

Shay interrupted him. "Forget about it. Let's just get back to the advice you were giving me. It's clear that I need help more than you do."

Liam was genuinely surprised by his host's graciousness and humility, traits he hadn't witnessed much during the past few hours. He would learn soon enough that it was a ruse.

DIRTY JOBS

"You know that TV show with the guy who spends a day with people who have horrible jobs?" Liam asked.

"Yeah, it's called *Dirty Jobs*. My kids love it. I think because about half the episodes have something to do with poop."

Liam laughed. "Perhaps. I like it because it shows people who seem to like their jobs even though they're doing something that others wouldn't want to do."

Shay tried his hardest not to be sarcastic. "Yeah, but I don't think my job entails anything close to shoveling alligator crap or cleaning out a sewer."

"And yet you don't want to do it."

"Okay, okay. I give," Shay relented sarcastically. "What part of my job don't I like to do?"

"Let's start with meetings."

"Okay. I admitted that I don't like meetings. I think they're a waste of time. But we already talked about that."

Liam smiled. "Yeah, we talked about it, but we haven't talked about *why*."

Shay sat back and thought about it. "I think we did talk about why. They're boring. They're a waste of time. Isn't that enough?"

"But if I asked Jackie or any of your other execs, they'd probably say that your staff meetings are boring and a waste of time too. Right?"

Shay shrugged, doing his best to hide any embarrassment. "Yeah, they probably would."

"So, bear with me here. Why are your meetings boring and a waste of time?"

Shay took a deep breath and stared at the stained-glass window at the other end of the dining room. Returning his eyes to Liam, he tried to explain.

"I guess that's just how meetings are. I don't know that I've ever really enjoyed meetings." He paused, realizing that his answer sounded a little pathetic. "I mean, I'm not saying that we shouldn't have them.

That's how I figure out what's going on in the business. But the way I see it, we get in there, we grind through the tedium, and we get out and get to work."

Liam nodded, wanting to avoid making Shay defensive. "I get that. I used to feel pretty much the same way."

"Really?"

Liam laughed. "Oh yeah. I sounded a lot like you."

"So what changed?"

"Well, the first thing that changed was being convinced by the consultants at Lighthouse that meetings are the most important work that a CEO does. And that bad meetings, boring meetings, ineffective meetings were my fault, and were lethal to the company. Until I really believed that, no meeting tactics or tools were going to make a difference."

Shay winced. "I don't know, man."

"As soon as I accepted that, it wasn't hard to make meetings interesting and effective."

Wanting to change the subject and find out if the rest of Liam's advice was better, Shay pretended to get on board. "So that's what Lighthouse helped you with?"

Liam nodded. "It's only part of it."

"What else?"

Liam smiled gently. "You're not going to like the next thing."

HUMAN

Shay actually laughed at Liam's warning. "Worse than meetings?"

"Yeah, I think so," Liam laughed back. "It takes more time and energy."

"Ouch," Shay responded. "Let me have it."

"It's about managing people, beginning with your team. Making sure they work together and aren't getting bogged down by politics and confusion."

Shay was relieved, and even a little excited. "Oh, you're talking about teambuilding. We have an annual event where we go off and do adventure activities and bond as a group." He seemed proud that he was on top of this one.

"No," Liam shook his head. "I'm talking about day-to-day development of your team. Getting them to be honest with each other and argue well. Making sure they can call each other on their bullshit when they're not focused on what they should be doing."

Shay didn't hesitate. "Oh, I hate that stuff. I don't tolerate it."

Liam wasn't sure what he meant, but wanted to be positive. "Good for you. So what do you do?"

"I tell people that I won't tolerate people being petty and political and acting like children."

"Does that work? If I asked Jackie or Karl if people were open and honest with each other or if there was a lot of politics on the team, what would they say?"

"Well," Shay suddenly seemed a little discouraged, "they'd probably say we have a lot of work to do in that area."

"And what are you doing about it?"

Shay seemed stuck. "What do *you* do about it?"

Liam laughed. "I have a lot of direct and uncomfortable conversations with people."

Shay's shoulders slumped. "Oh, I hate that."

After an awkward moment, the two CEOs started laughing out loud, in an almost pathetic way.

"Well," Liam assured him, "the good news is that very few people in the world like to do it."

Shay nodded his agreement.

Liam continued. "And that's why I said before that you are supposed to have the most painful job in the company." He paused and let it sink in. "See, if the CEO isn't confronting people about their issues, as unpleasant as that might be, he can't expect anyone else to. It sucks, but it has to happen."

"Like with Jackie," Shay conceded.

"Yeah, like with Jackie." Liam confirmed. "And anyone else who needs to be confronted."

With a sudden sense of energy, Shay raised himself up in his chair and cheerfully asked Liam, "So, are you going to tell me that you actually like doing this too?"

"Well," Liam tried to choose his words carefully, "I don't know that I'd say I like it. I mean, every time I have to do it I'm tempted to avoid it."

"What kind of stuff are we talking about here?" Shay wanted to know.

Liam thought about it for a few moments. Suddenly he laughed painfully, calling to mind a recent experience. "A few weeks ago, I had to ask my head of sales not to hum during meetings."

"Did you say *hum?*"

Liam nodded.

"Oh come on!" Shay protested. "That's ridiculous. I thought you were talking about business stuff—missing deadlines, pissing off customers. *Humming?*"

Liam shrugged and laughed. "I know. It sounds strange. But it was driving people crazy. It was really distracting."

Shay just laughed, but now in a slightly judgmental way.

Liam didn't back down. "I also get on people when they check their phones during meetings. I've had to tell my head of sales to talk less and ask more questions. And more than a few times I've had to confront team members who I thought weren't spending enough time managing their own people." He paused. "And, yes, I have to be ready to call them on their numbers and their deadlines. But that's a lot easier than the behavioral stuff."

"I guess," Shay admitted. "But it's not as important."

Liam shot back. "Okay, what about Jackie?"

"What about her?"

"What would it be worth to you and your team if you could get her to be more thoughtful and diplomatic?"

Shay shook his head. "I don't know. But if she doesn't figure out how to cut expenses by four percent next year, I might have to fire her."

Liam frowned.

"I'm kidding. What I'm trying to say is that if she does her job well, I don't care if she has bad breath, farts during meetings, and sings show tunes in the lunch room."

Even Liam couldn't keep from laughing. "But you're ignoring the impact she's having on others. And it's going to affect her ability to get them to cut their budgets and do their jobs. You have to see that, Shay."

"Maybe. But I am not going to go around treating my grown-up executives like a bunch of middle school kids. We can all be big enough to deal with people's quirks without making a big deal out of it."

Liam just sat and listened.

When Shay saw that he wasn't arguing, he decided to seek common ground.

"Hey, isn't it possible that there is more than one way to skin a cat? Maybe we just have different ways."

Liam nodded, but not enthusiastically.

Shay doubled down. "Listen, if I manage to put together a big sales deal with a strategic partner, or I find a way to acquire a company at a discount, or if I land a whale of a client through my sales and negotiation skills, then I think I'm more than making up for the difference between letting people like Jackie be a little rough around the edges."

"Well," Liam offered gently, "perhaps I do have a different way to skin a cat."

Liam decided to back off for the moment, and the two CEOs spent the next half hour talking about the challenges of their businesses, dealing with competition and government regulations and other industry-specific matters. It was the most pleasant part of their time together so far.

Finally, the waitress came and laid the check on the table. Liam thanked her and reached for it.

"No way, buddy," Shay objected. "You come up here and give me all this free advice, and the least I can do is pay …" he paused looking at the check, "twenty-three dollars and fifteen cents for lunch."

He left thirty dollars on the table and, looking at his watch, announced with more cheer than Liam thought was warranted. "Let's continue this conversation back in my office."

Liam had no idea about what would be waiting for him there.

TRAP

On the way back to the office, Shay made a call to his assistant, Rita, to whom he said only five words. "I'll be there in ten."

Liam wondered why their arrival time mattered but dismissed it without any thought.

As they pulled up to the office and climbed out of the car, Shay made a comment that raised Liam's suspicions.

"You know, I really respect you, Liam, and appreciate you coming up here. I hope you know that."

A little confused, Liam paused before shutting his door. "Uh, okay. Thanks."

When they entered the office, Rita was waiting for them. "Joe and Kerry are in the conference room upstairs."

"Thanks, Rita."

As they climbed the stairs leading to the nicest conference room in the building, Liam asked, "Are you expecting someone?"

Shay announced confidently, "There are some people here I want you to meet."

At the top of the stairs, Liam could see a man and a woman in business suits looking out on the San Francisco Bay.

"Thanks for coming on such short notice, you guys," Shay announced, as though he were talking to close friends.

They turned, and Shay introduced everyone. "This is Liam, the CEO of Del Mar Alarm."

The man spoke first. "We've heard really good things about you, Liam."

As he and the woman shook Liam's hand, Shay introduced them. "Liam, this is Joe Werblun and Kerry Ryder."

"You can call me Joey."

Liam was thoroughly confused about why they were there. "And what do you guys do?" he asked.

Joey looked at Shay. "Oh, you guys haven't talked about this yet?"

Shay shook his head. "No, I thought it would be good to wait until now."

Kerry seemed a little hesitant, but finally jumped in. "Well, we're from Bayside Partners. We're Shay's private equity firm."

Liam was puzzled and looked at Shay.

Not able to delay the announcement any longer, Shay looked down at his feet and then back up at Liam. "I want to buy your company, my friend."

He waited to see how the British CEO would react.

But Liam only frowned, as though he couldn't process what he was hearing.

Shay continued. "We're going to make you a very rich man, Liam."

Shay and his investors moved to the conference table to sit down, and Liam followed them in something of a catatonic state. When they were seated, Joey went first.

"I know this is sudden. Shay just called us this morning. But the way he described your company, and the idea that he could put together a sizable regional rival to All-American Alarm, made us jump at the opportunity."

Liam began to emerge from his haze, and his face was growing red. "What in the world makes you think this is doable?"

"Well," Joey explained politely, "Golden Gate Security is flush with cash. They have much more than you guys in San Diego." He paused and seemed a little hesitant to go on. "And, well, we called a few members of your board."

"What did they say?" Liam asked desperately. "I can't imagine that they—"

Kerry interrupted. "Actually, I spoke to Tom and Kathryn, and they said there was no way they would approve of anything like this."

Liam was visibly relieved. "Right. I didn't think—"

This time Joey interrupted. "Until we told them how much we were prepared to pay. That seemed to change their attitude."

"And what about your board?" Liam pressed Shay. "Do they think this is a good idea?"

Shay nodded. "When I shared your numbers with them, they told me to move fast."

"Which is why we're here," Kerry explained. "We think there is a window of opportunity that may close sooner than we'd like. And then we're going to approach two of the larger security companies in Los Angeles and Phoenix to see if we can't create a real West Coast threat to All-American Alarm."

Liam barely nodded his head, but only to indicate that he was hearing what Kerry had said. His shock was giving way to resignation. "You don't expect me to commit to anything right now, do you?"

Joey laughed. "No, no. Of course not. We came here to show you how serious we are. Shay thought it would be better than a call or a Skype meeting. But we would like to accelerate this and try to close by the end of Golden Gate's fiscal year."

"That gives us two and a half months," Shay explained.

Liam nodded dispassionately. "Right. So is there anything specific that you want from me today?"

Joey and Kerry looked at one another, and then turned back to Liam shaking their heads.

"No," Kerry explained. "At this point we have to do some due diligence and paperwork before we can present you with anything concrete. We'll let you know when we're ready to talk again, and if all goes well, we'd like to go down there for a site visit sometime soon."

Liam nodded his head again, trying to force a smile. "Okay then. It was nice meeting you." He didn't mean it.

Clearly getting the message that Liam had nothing else to say, the well-dressed investors stood, exchanged handshakes with Shay, and left the room. Shay returned to the table, a little nervous.

"Okay, I know this is a bit of a shock, Liam."

Liam was stunned. "You think so?" He responded with a mix of anger and sarcasm.

Shay went on. "But I think it's the right thing to do at the right time."

Silence.

Finally, Liam spoke, barely containing his emotions. "Shay, it would be very easy for me to be furious with you right now." He paused. "In fact, if I still had the boxing gloves that my parents kept in our garage for me and my brother, I'd be tempted to lace them up right now in this conference room and beat the bloody crap out of you." He paused again. "But that's not my thing."

Shay smiled sheepishly and uncomfortably. "Well, I'm certainly glad for that."

Liam didn't respond to the poor attempt at humor. "And you should be really glad that I didn't say in front of your partners what I'm about to say to you right now."

"I appreciate that," Shay offered, though he didn't seem to know exactly what Liam was getting at.

"Good. Because we need to continue the talk we were having at lunch. And if you thought I was direct there, you're going to be in for a surprise."

The smile on Shay's face faded.

GLOVES OFF

"Do you really think our conversation is still relevant?" Shay asked Liam. "I mean, given what's going on?"

Liam took a deep breath. "You really don't get it, do you?"

"I guess not," Shay responded, unconvincingly.

"Do you think you are going to be able to take what we've done at Del Mar and keep it going?" He didn't wait for a response. "Do you think that our numbers are unrelated to the things I've been telling you about?"

Shay didn't respond, but his demeanor seemed to indicate that he disagreed with what Liam was saying.

"Your numbers up here are worse than ours because you aren't doing your job." He stood up from his chair. "You don't even like your job."

"Wait a second," Shay interrupted, slightly agitated now.

Liam didn't stop. "You run terrible meetings, and you don't care. You don't manage your people or your team, and you don't care. You can't have uncomfortable conversations with your people. You spend most of your time doing the things you feel like doing."

Shay offered no rebuttal.

Liam went on. "Don't you realize that your job is to do things that no one else in the company can do?"

Shay didn't seem to have an answer. Finally, he offered a pathetic response. "Maybe I prefer to delegate."

"Come on, man." Liam raised his voice. "You're not delegating. You're abdicating."

In a matter of minutes, Shay's disposition had shifted from confident to apologetic to defensive. "Is that all you've got? I don't like meetings, and I don't like to babysit people?"

"No, it's not all I've got. But it's not about meetings and babysitting. It's about keeping your people engaged in the most important conversations, and it's about holding them to higher standards." He paused. "But I guess it makes sense when your standards for yourself are so low."

Now Shay was angry. "That's bullshit. I work my ass off for this company. And just because I'm out-maneuvering you doesn't give you the right to ..." he paused searching for the right words, "be an asshole."

Liam didn't respond. Silence.

When he was convinced that Shay was done speaking for the moment, he finally spoke. "You're right." He paused. "And you're wrong."

Shay seemed neither pleased nor angry, so Liam went on. "I have no right to be an asshole, and my last comment was harsh."

Shay was still angry, but shrugged as if to say *it's not that big of a deal*. "So what am I wrong about?"

"You're not going to want to hear this, but I have to tell you anyway." He paused before finishing. "You might be working hard, but you're not doing it for the company."

"What the hell does that mean?" Shay wanted to know.

Knowing that his adversary might now punch him for what he was about to say, Liam responded. "You're doing it for yourself."

To Liam's great surprise, and relief, Shay didn't seem as angry as he did sad. In fact, all he said was, "Tell me more about that."

And that was when Liam decided there was still hope for a breakthrough.

JUGULAR

Liam returned to the table and sat down next to Shay. "Okay, you need to pay attention here. I'm not going to pull any punches."

"Have you been pulling punches? Because if that's what you call pulling—"

Liam interrupted. "No, I haven't. But I could've been bloody mean."

"Okay," Shay responded, with a strange mixture of confusion and trust.

"Here it is in a nutshell. You are doing the things you like to do. You aren't doing the things your company needs you to do. And that is why your company's performance is so far behind ours." He paused. "You need to believe me here. I'm telling you the truth."

Shay took it in.

"And in a few minutes, I'm going to ask you one question. I'll need you to answer it honestly. You will have to think about it. It's extremely important."

"Why don't you just ask me now."

Liam shook his head. "I think you'll be able to answer it better a little later."

Shay smiled. "You're a strange guy, Liam. I mean, one minute you want to punch me in the face. The next you're trying to help me."

"Oh, I'd still like to punch you," Liam explained. "But I think we can still figure this out and prevent a tragedy."

Shay stopped smiling. "Or maybe I can convince you that it wouldn't be a tragedy."

"That would make me very happy," Liam said.

Then he went to the whiteboard and wrote the following:

Things I avoided when I was a bad CEO

Running great meetings

Managing my executive team

Managing my executives as individuals

Having difficult conversations with people

Constantly communicating and
repeating key messages to employees

Liam turned and saw Shay wince as he read the items on the board.

"See, you have to stop doing that. If you look at these kinds of things with dread, you're through."

Shay shook his head. "Okay, what else?"

He circled *Managing my executives* on the board.

Shay frowned. "You already covered that one."

"No, that was about confronting people, including them, about uncomfortable things. What I'm talking about here is knowing enough about what they're working on to provide whatever support they need."

"I think I do that pretty well. You remember what Jackie told you this morning, right?"

"Yeah, but I think it's different," Liam explained. "Why don't you explain what you're thinking."

"Well," Shay thought about it, "she said that I'm hands off until the shit hits the fan and I have to dive in and take over."

"Okay, here's my question for you."

"The big question?"

"No, a little one. But it's key for managing." He paused. "When the shit hits the fan, as you say, are you usually surprised? Or do you see it coming and—"

Shay interrupted. "I'm always surprised. And I'm not happy, which is why they don't want me diving in."

"So when you say you're hands off, you really mean it?"

Shay nodded. "Oh yeah. I hire people who have lots of experience and who shouldn't need to be managed."

"Why do you think they don't need to be managed?" Liam asked. "Or for that matter, why anyone wouldn't need to be managed?"

"I don't know. If I'm paying these people as much as I'm paying them, I think it's reasonable to expect them to manage themselves. They're big boys and girls."

"So what exactly do you think management is?"

"Well, it's about goal setting and progress reviews and that kind of stuff. That's what I did for twenty years. Now that I'm CEO, it's different."

"How?" Liam asked with the patience of a prosecuting attorney.

"I don't know. Listen, if a CEO has to look over his executives' shoulders, he's hiring the wrong people. I'm not going to micromanage a fifty-two-year-old operations executive. And I think my people prefer my approach."

"Not if they fail."

"If they start to fail, I'll jump in and help them."

"You mean you'll do their job, especially if it's in marketing or sales or M&A."

"Call it what you want. I help them."

Liam pursued a separate line of questioning. "So, during your meetings—"

"Back to meetings?" Shay interrupted, laughing sarcastically.

"Back to meetings." Liam looked at the whiteboard as though he were searching for something in the words there. "Tell me exactly what happens during your staff meetings."

Shay took a deep, frustrated breath.

"What do you mean?"

"How do you run them? What do you do first, second, third?"

Shay shook his head in frustration, but complied. "Well, I usually start by asking Jackie to take us through the numbers. Depending on what she tells us, I then ask a lot of questions. If we're lagging in service revenue, I'm asking Karl about it. If it's an expense issue, I'm asking whatever department is over budget. Then everyone goes around the table and gives us an update about what they're working on. And maybe we talk about any big issues that are up in the air."

"Like what?"

"It could be anything from a large new customer we're trying to land, or a new advertising campaign or ..." he paused, "I don't know, planning the Christmas party. Whatever is happening at that moment."

"What about technology or HR or operations?"

Shay shook his head. "I am not a technology guy. Thank God I have Ben. And Margaret handles ops. And the HR stuff is usually so touchy-feely."

"Again, you just deal with the stuff you know about."

Shay shrugged, then nodded.

"The stuff you enjoy."

He nodded again, but a little less enthusiastically. And then he thought of something. "Hey, I thought you were telling me earlier that you don't have time to get involved in your executives' departments, and that all your time is taken up being the CEO. Now you're telling me I need to micromanage people."

Liam shook his head. "First, I didn't say I'm doing my people's jobs. I'm just coaching them, making sure they have a good plan and that I know about any big issue before it's too late to do something about it. That's not micromanagement."

"Potato, Potahto."

Liam shook his head. "No. It's management. The only people who call it micromanagement are employees who don't want to be held accountable."

Shay actually seemed to accept that logic.

Liam finished his thought. "And CEOs who don't want to have to manage at all."

"Ouch," Shay teased sarcastically.

"Hear me out. Just because someone is in his forties or fifties or sixties and has lots of experience doesn't mean he doesn't need to be managed. It's not a form of punishment or the sign of a lack of trust. It's the benefit of direction and guidance. I mean, the best football player in the world needs coaching." ✓

"Are you talking about football or soccer?" Shay asked, teasing again.

Liam wasn't in the mood to indulge Shay's poor attempt at humor. "You know what I'm saying. The best golfers and tennis players and other athletes pay people lots of money to coach them. Why in the world would you think a head of marketing or sales or finance doesn't need it? And that's to say nothing of managing them as a team."

Shay shrugged.

Liam persisted, more intense now. "I'm serious, Shay. It's a sign of neglect for a CEO to stop managing people just because he can get away with it."

"I'm sorry if I still seem skeptical. I guess I really thought that your management consultant gave you something a little more ..." he paused searching for the right words, "concrete. This is all pretty soft."

Liam took a deep breath. "Can we take a ten-minute break? I need to make a call of my own."

Shay looked at his watch. "Sure. We still have plenty of time before the end of the day, and I need to have a quick call with my board. Let's meet back here at two."

As Shay left, Liam said a quick prayer that Amy would be available.

SKYPE

When Shay returned, he saw Liam doing a video call on his laptop with a woman. Catching Liam's eye, he motioned for permission to enter the room.

Liam waved him in.

"Here he is now, Amy." Liam said to a woman on the computer screen.

Then, turning to Shay, he introduced them. "Shay, this is Amy Stirling, who you spoke with briefly last week. She is one of the principals over at Lighthouse, and the lead consultant who worked with us over the past three years."

Shay sat down in front of the computer and greeted the consultant confidently. "Hi, Amy. It's nice to meet you. I certainly appreciate Liam sharing what you did for him."

"Do you?" Amy asked, without any sense of sarcasm or judgment.

"Well, yeah. I mean, it's always good to learn new things." Shay responded politely.

"I've only got about ten minutes here before I have to go back in with my client. So I'll be direct, if that's okay."

"Please."

"Well, Liam seems to think that you're not all that interested in learning new things. Perhaps he hasn't done a good job of portraying what we did with him at Del Mar. Does that sound right?"

Shay didn't answer the question directly. "Amy, I'll be direct too. I just don't see how all this stuff about meetings and managing people and having uncomfortable conversations can possibly make the difference between success and failure. It's not that I don't see any value in it. But not every CEO goes about his or her job that way."

Amy took it in. "Okay, you're not the first CEO who said that. In fact, you sound a lot like Liam did a few years ago."

Liam nodded at Shay as if to say *I told you so.*

She went on. "Let me make this as clear as possible. If you're having bad meetings, you're making bad decisions. There is no getting around that. And you're almost certainly not talking about all the right things."

Shay seemed like he was about to respond, but Amy went on.

"And if your meetings are bad, then there is a very, very good chance that your executives are having bad meetings with their teams. And it cascades from there. And the person who is responsible for making your meetings effective is you—no one else. You can't delegate that job. It's yours and yours alone."

"I know. I know." Shay said defensively. "That's what Liam's been telling me. And he said I'm not managing my people and not having difficult conversations. I get it. I just don't buy it. That's not who I am. It's not what I'm good at."

"Did Liam get to the last thing you can't delegate?"

"I don't know. Is there more?"

"Yeah. You also have to be the primary communication tool."

"Well, I'm pretty involved in marketing and—"

Even over Skype, Amy was able to interrupt Shay. "No, I mean internal communication. With employees."

"Yeah, I do that. We have a big kickoff with all the VPs at the beginning of the year. And I do a video thing we call the "State of the Union" right after that. And I try to visit the field offices once a quarter. I'm not bad at that."

"That's great. But I'm talking about being a constant, incessant reminder of the company's purpose, strategy, values, priorities. I like to say that you're not only the CEO, you're the CRO."

Before Shay could ask, she explained.

"The chief reminding officer. Prospective employees. New employees. Current employees. Constant reminders and updates and stories. There is no such thing as communicating too much about the important stuff."

Shay wasn't excited about what he was hearing, but he wanted to redeem himself in the eyes of this supposed expert. "I send out a quarterly business report, with key customer updates and sales numbers."

"That's fine," Amy explained. "But those are things your head of sales and CFO can do. I'm talking about the more fundamental stuff. Keeping people focused and aligned and engaged around what they're doing and why they're doing it."

Shay took a deep, frustrated breath. "Listen, Amy. I'm sure that you and your firm do wonderful work. And I'm sure that many companies out there are a good fit for your message."

As much as he wanted to yell at Shay, Liam kept his cool and let him continue.

"But I just don't think my time is best spent doing all this stuff you're talking about. I'm a deal-maker. I'm good at putting together deals, explaining why the Golden Gate solution is right for our customers, and coming in when things get hairy and convincing them to go with us. That is a huge part of our success."

Silence. Liam would later learn that even Amy was fighting off the urge to get angry at Shay.

Finally, Amy pulled her last and most dangerous arrow from her quiver. "I have a question for you, Shay. And it's the most important one of all. I don't want you to answer right away but to really give it thought. And please be completely honest."

Shay looked at Liam, suddenly a little excited. "Is this the big question you were going to ask me earlier?"

Liam nodded.

He turned back to the screen. "Okay."

Amy continued. "Shay, why did you want to become a CEO?" She paused. "Or perhaps a better way to ask it is this: Why do you *still* want to be the CEO of Golden Gate Alarm?"

"Golden Gate Security," he corrected her.

"Sorry. Anyway, take a minute to think about that. I'm really, really curious about your answer."

He started to speak, and she cut him off. "Please take a full minute to think about it before answering."

Shay looked out the window and stretched, the same way his dog did every morning. No one spoke. Shay seemed to be concentrating on his answer.

After about forty-five seconds, Shay broke the silence. "I have an answer."

Amy nodded her head. "Okay. Go ahead."

"I don't know," Shay said matter-of-factly.

"You don't know?" Liam asked incredulously.

Amy was smiling on the screen.

BREAKTHROUGH

Shay shook his head at Liam. "No, I really don't know."

Shay paused, frowning, as though he were simultaneously puzzled and confident. Then turning back toward Amy, he explained.

"I mean, how do you answer that question? I'm driven. I want to succeed. I like to compete. I want to improve. I guess ever since I started working I knew that I would one day be the CEO of something. It's the prize that keeps you going."

Neither Amy nor Liam responded right away.

Shay turned back to Liam. "Why did *you* want to be a CEO?"

"For the same reason you did."

Shay seemed confused, so Liam explained.

"But that's not why I want to be the CEO of Del Mar Alarm now."

"What do you mean?"

Now Amy jumped in. "Listen guys. I'm so sorry but I have to get back into my off-site with a client. I think you can handle it from here."

Though Liam wasn't sure she was right, he agreed with Amy and thanked her for her time. And she was gone.

Liam gathered himself and tried to be as strong and confident as possible.

"Shay, I want to be the CEO of Del Mar because I see my job as a responsibility and a sacrifice. You're the CEO of Golden Gate because you see your job as a reward. Like you, I used to think that way—that being a CEO was a reward for a lifetime of hard work, which meant it was about getting to do what I wanted because I had earned the right to do so. That's why I failed so miserably in England. And I was about to do the same thing in San Diego. And that's what you're doing here." He paused before finishing. "And the thing is, it might work for you, but it never works for the people or the organization you're supposed to be leading."

Shay was neither agreeing with nor dismissing Liam, who went on.

"All those responsibilities and activities we've been talking about today are just a function of our motives for being a leader. We can talk all day about *what* we're supposed to do, but if we don't understand *why* we're leading in the first place, none of it will make sense."

Liam saw the look on Shay's face change just slightly, as though a lightbulb, albeit a dim one, went off in his head. So he continued.

"Shay, when I have to dive into the middle of a petty political issue between the sales and engineering teams, or when I have to give someone their final warning about having to change their behavior, or when I have to call a meeting after hours to deal with an emergency issue, or when I have to give the same bloody orientation speech to another group of new employees, or when I have to go out to the installers and remind them that they're the front line of the company and everyone is relying on them, or when I have to," he paused, "do anything that no one else can do because they're not the CEO, I smile and thank God that I am making a difference. I have the worst and best, loneliest and most social, most appreciated and most thankless job in the company. And I do that job with pride and without complaint. Because that was what I signed up for, even if I didn't realize it until Amy told me."

Shay sat there silently. Liam couldn't read him at all.

Finally, Shay nodded his head and spoke.

"You're a good guy, Liam."

Liam was confused.

"Your coming up here was as generous as it was bizarre. And I mean that in the best way." Shay seemed sincere.

Liam acknowledged the unique compliment.

Shay took a deep breath. "Let's do this. On Monday morning, why don't we talk—"

Liam interrupted. "I have my leadership team meetings from ten to noon."

"Okay, then let's talk right after lunch on Monday, if that works. I won't say anything to my employees here. And I'd appreciate it if you didn't with yours. Let's take the weekend to let all this settle and see where we are. Okay?"

Liam nodded. "Yeah, I guess so. Okay."

The two very different CEOs shook hands and called it an early day.

Shay had no idea that his next lesson would come before the weekend began.

AUTHORITY

By the time Shay made it back to his office, his cell phone was ringing. It was Dani calling about dinner.

"Hey, the boys are sleeping over at friends' houses tonight."

"All of them?"

"Yeah. Let's go on a date."

"Okay, you say where and when, and I'll be there."

"I want Maria's," Dani declared. "I haven't been there in months."

"Ooh. I went there for lunch."

Dani begged. "Oh, can't you go again? You can get something different. Please."

"Okay, but you're buying."

"Deal. See you at five-thirty?" Then she caught herself. "Oh, how was your day with Liam Alcott?" She exaggerated his name and added a slight English accent to it.

"I'll tell you at dinner. Five-thirty."

Dani was already seated at the restaurant when Shay arrived. She was at the table next to the one where Shay and Liam had been five hours earlier.

As soon as Shay sat down, she began. "So, tell me about your day."

Shay was surprised by her enthusiasm. "You're awfully excited."

"Well, Rita told me that things got really heated. She didn't know why, but she thought it might be big."

"Well, let's just say it didn't go the way Liam probably thought it would."

"Was he an ass?" Dani caught herself. "I'm sorry. I should be nicer. Was he as pompous as you thought he would be?"

Shay paused and winced. "Oh, I hate to admit it, but no. I honestly can't say he was a pompous ass, at all. In fact, he was a pretty decent guy."

Dani was pleased. "Okay. That's good, right?"

Shay shrugged. "Yeah, I guess so."

"You guess so? What do you mean?"

"It's complicated."

"Okay, buster," Dani scolded her husband. "You're going to start from the beginning and tell me exactly what happened. And slow down for the heated part."

For the next half hour, Shay recounted the day in as much detail as he could. Everything from the financial comparison to the initial call to his investors to lunch at Maria's (and the fact that they sat at the adjacent table) and the big meeting back in the conference room.

Dani listened attentively. But when Shay was finished, she seemed to have lost her sense of excitement.

"What's wrong?" her husband asked.

"Nothing. I don't know."

"You seem a little confused, or disappointed."

Dani glanced over at the empty table next to theirs. "I don't know."

"Come on," Shay encouraged her. "You usually know."

"Okay," she said, frowning, "don't take this the wrong way. Because I might be seeing this all wrong."

Shay nodded.

"There is one thing that isn't making sense to me. And it's weird."

She was clearly hesitant to say what she was thinking.

"Come on, lady. Spill it."

She smiled. "Okay. I'm just wondering if this acquisition is such a good idea."

Shay responded quickly. "Listen, if we can pull three or four good regional security companies together, we will make it much, much harder for All-American to—"

Dani interrupted her husband. "I know. It makes strategic sense. I get that."

She paused yet again.

"So what's the problem?" he asked.

"Well, how is Liam feeling about all this? I mean, he didn't come up here to sell you his company."

Shay shrugged. "I mean, he's not thrilled. But this is how business works sometimes, especially in an evolving market. And Liam's either going to become very rich and leave, or become very rich and stick around to help out. Trust me, he's going to be fine."

Dani didn't seem completely satisfied. "Okay. But honey, do you really want to run a bigger company?"

Shay shrugged. "Why not? It's just a different size."

"But do *you* want to run a bigger company? I mean, are you really enjoying what you're doing now?"

He frowned, a little confused.

She went on. "Since you've become CEO, I think you've complained more about work than you did in the last ten years. Are you having fun?"

"Sure," he responded, much too quickly. "I mean, it's hard. Being the CEO is a lonely job."

"I know. But tonight, you seem so excited because you're doing this big deal."

"And what's the problem with that?"

"Are you going to be excited doing all the stuff that it requires? Or are you just going to keep looking for another acquisition? What are you really looking forward to here?"

Shay looked over at the table next to him, and sagged in his chair. "This is so weird."

"What?" Dani was concerned.

"You sound like the woman from Liam's consulting firm."

"What do you mean?"

"Well, she asked me why I wanted to be a CEO. And I thought it was a stupid question."

Dani tried to reassure her husband. "Well, I can see why you thought that. I mean, you've worked hard all these years and, well, it seems logical." She paused. "Right?"

Shay nodded but didn't seem to mean it. "Yeah. But if you're asking me the same question and …" He didn't finish the sentence.

"Okay, let's answer that question together. Why do you want to be a CEO?" Then she corrected herself. "Or maybe the better question should be 'Why do you want to do what a CEO does?'"

Shay looked at her like she had just told him there was no Santa Claus. "What did you just say?"

"I said you should ask yourself why you like doing what a CEO does. The day-to-day stuff."

"Why did you ask it that way?"

"Well, remember when I was teaching fourth grade at St. Mary's before we joined the parish? Remember when the principal's job opened up and someone asked me to consider applying?"

Shay nodded, though he was somewhat ashamed that he hadn't been as attentive as he should have been back then.

Dani continued. "Well, at first I thought 'Heck yeah, I should apply. I'm one of the best teachers at the school.'"

"You were *the* best teacher at that school."

"You're biased. Anyway, when I thought about what principals do all day and what I loved about being a teacher, I realized that it wasn't right for me. Up until that point, I always assumed that I'd be a principal. But I realized it was an ego thing. I really just wanted to be in a classroom, teaching. Not managing teachers and going to meetings."

Shay was suddenly intense. Out of nowhere he asked, "Hey, a participle is a verb, right?"

Dani was confused. "What?"

"You know. A participle is—"

She interrupted him. "Yes, I know what a participle is. Why are you asking me that in the middle of this conversation?"

So he explained the difference between a chief *executive* officer and a chief *executing* officer.

Dani was nodding her head. "Oh, that's good. Yes, it really should be the chief *executing* officer. It's about *doing* the job, not just *having* the job."

At that point Shay dropped his margarita and spilled it directly into his basket of tortilla chips.

As they cleaned up the mess, which was largely contained within the basket of soggy chips, Dani could see that Shay was upset about more than the spill.

"What's going on, Shay?"

"I think I have a problem."

DESSERT

For the next forty-five minutes, Shay and his wife came to terms with the reality that he had never really embraced what CEOs do. It was almost as jarring for her as it was for him, having watched him climb the ladder for two decades.

By the time they had finished eating—Shay would later admit that he never tasted the food that night—they did something that they had never done during any of their dinners at Maria's. They ordered dessert.

They had always joked about flan, wondering if anyone actually ordered it. But here they were, asking the waitress to bring them a plate of the gelatinous goo. By the time it arrived, Shay was coming to terms with his situation and could actually taste what he was eating.

"This is actually really good," he declared to Dani.

She laughed. "You seem a bit lighter than you did a few minutes ago."

"Yeah, I guess I'm seeing the light at the end of the tunnel here, and it feels like a relief."

"Tell me more," Dani asked as she wrestled flan onto her spoon,

"I don't know. I can't see how this is going to play out. But I think it's time I forced myself to grow a little."

Dani chuckled.

"What?" Shay wanted to know.

"It just sounds like the end of a Hallmark movie. 'I think it's time I forced myself to grow a little.'"

Shay laughed. "Hey, since when did you become a cynic?" He threw his napkin at Dani. "Maybe I'm maturing here."

"I'm sorry, honey. I'm proud of you," she said sincerely. And then couldn't resist saying, "I can't wait to see how you look in your big boy pants."

He laughed. "Let's get out of here and have a weekend. I'm tired of thinking about work."

PROCESSING

Over the course of the next few weeks, Shay and the investors dove into the details of the acquisition, which meant that Shay had plenty of opportunities to interact with Liam and his executive team on a tactical level. Much to Shay's surprise, Liam found a way to be professional and productive. A few of his leaders in San Diego were a little less cooperative.

Through it all, Liam continued to pound Shay, always privately, when he saw him put his own needs ahead of the company's. "What do I have to lose?" he even admitted to Shay on one occasion.

On a personal level, Shay felt like he was riding a roller coaster. Forcing himself to think about his job differently, he found himself excited one moment about the prospect of Golden Gate becoming a more substantial entity in the market and down the next moment for reasons he didn't completely understand.

But there was little time for self-analysis, given the pace at which they were trying to execute the merger.

And to make things more difficult, Shay felt the need to present himself to his board members, investors, and new employees as a confident, self-assured leader. By the time the deal was on the verge of completion, he was exhausted by having to play that role and knew that the upcoming week of announcements was going to be a tough one.

"Instead of going to business school," he told Dani on Sunday night before bed, "I feel like I should have studied acting."

Neither of them laughed.

"Pray for guidance," Dani offered. "And courage."

Shay was too tired to sort out what that might mean.

DECISION SCIENCE

On Monday morning, Shay set up a video call for himself, Liam, and one board member from each of their companies. Joey, Shay's private equity guy, was his board representative, and he was in the room with Shay. Liam invited Kathryn Petersen, a retired executive, who was in Liam's office representing Del Mar's board.

When the call began, Shay introduced Joey and Kathryn and laid out the agenda for the call.

"Okay, we're here to clarify some of the last details in the acquisition. I want to get clear on what the deal would look like and how it would play out financially, strategically, and organizationally."

Shay seemed more confident and commanding than Liam had seen him be at any time on that Friday a few weeks earlier.

Kathryn spoke first. "Can we start with the organizational piece?"

Shay looked at Joey and they nodded at one another. "Sure."

Kathryn continued. "I'm wondering how you—"

Shay interrupted her. "Excuse me, Kathryn. But before you ask any questions, let me lay out what the executive team would look like, and we can go from there."

Even on video Shay could tell that Kathryn seemed a little miffed by his directness and control.

"That's fine," she said unenthusiastically.

"Okay," Shay began, "I realize this is going to seem like it's coming out of the blue, especially at this late stage. But it's become clear to me that Liam should be the CEO."

Everyone on the call, including Joey sitting next to him, was stunned. But no one spoke, so Shay continued.

"Liam's acceptance of that role is not contingent on what I'm about to ask him. He has every right to deny my request." He paused. "But I'd like him to consider me as a candidate to run marketing or strategy."

Finally, Joey spoke. "So you're going to acquire his company and he's going to run it?" He seemed more confused than disappointed.

Shay nodded. "Yeah. It's clear that he is better at all the leadership and management stuff. And if we're going to be acquiring two more firms in the next two years, we need him focused on building the organization like he did at Del Mar. I can focus on integrating our marketing efforts and finding the next few acquisitions."

Kathryn was now smiling. Liam wasn't.

Liam finally spoke. "Well, first, I'd be lying if I didn't say that I'm shocked." He took a deep breath.

Shay nodded.

Liam continued. "Second, you know that if you worked for me, I would require you to be the kind of manager and leader that I expect my people to be?"

Shay nodded again, smiling. "Yeah, I realize that. If you could be patient with me, I think I could do it."

Liam went on. "And third, I'm still not convinced that this merger is the right move, financially and strategically. I mean, we're holding our own against All-American down here in San Diego, and I'm concerned that a larger organization would not be able to maintain the kind of customer intimacy that provides our key point of differentiation from a large national company."

"Wow," Shay remarked. "You're smarter than you sound."

"It's the accent," Liam joked.

Everyone laughed, but genuinely, not in a sitcom kind of way.

For the next ninety-five minutes, the four executives debated the viability of the merger. Liam changed his mind three times based on insights from Shay and Kathryn.

At the end of the meeting, Shay thanked everyone for their time and energy. "This was a fantastic conversation, and because of that, I think we've come to the right decision."

SAN DIEGO

Three months after the deal was closed, Shay and his family moved to Southern California. By the end of the summer, Dani would say that demoting himself was the best decision her husband had ever made. He was enjoying his work for the first time in a year and learning more about managing and leading than he had at any time in his career.

Late one night after they had put their boys to bed and were closing down their new home, she nervously asked him a question.

"Do you want to be a CEO again someday?"

Without hesitation he replied, "No."

Dani was surprised. Until he finished.

"But I'm starting to think that in a few years I might be ready to do what a CEO does."

The Lesson

INTRODUCTION

BACKGROUND

Most of the books I've written relate in one way or another to helping leaders make their organizations healthier, which essentially comes down to reducing politics, confusion, and dysfunction and increasing clarity, alignment, and productivity. As you might guess, just about every leader I've met would like his or her organization to become healthier. Why wouldn't they?

Unfortunately, over the course of my career I've come to realize that some leaders fail to achieve organizational health because they possess an almost unconscious unwillingness to do the difficult tasks and confront the challenging situations that are required to bring it about. This unwillingness flows from a flawed—and dangerous—motivation for becoming a leader.

As passionately as I feel about all this, I almost didn't write this book because one of my heroes didn't agree with its premise.

A few years ago, I had the opportunity to spend two days in my office with one of the best leaders in modern American business. Alan Mulally ran the commercial division of Boeing, where he led the launch of the 777 airplane, and then went on to revive the Ford Motor Company in one of the most amazing corporate turnarounds of modern business history. During my two-day session with Alan, he said something that jarred me. "There is one thing in your book *The Advantage* that I disagree with, Pat. It's the part where you say that leadership requires suffering." I was puzzled, so he explained.

✓ "Leadership is a privilege," he announced. "It shouldn't be seen as something sacrificial. It's a joy." And that's when I realized why Alan was such an amazing leader. See, he *really* believed what he was saying. And more importantly, he believed that everyone else believed it too!

So I responded, "Alan, you're not in Kansas anymore" (which was particularly fun to tell him, because he was actually raised in Lawrence, Kansas). I explained to him that most leaders today don't generally see their role as a privilege or a duty. They see it as a right and a reward. Once I explained this to Alan and shared stories about so many of the leaders I've encountered who operated this way (most notably in Silicon Valley and Wall Street), he understood where I was coming from. The fact is, far too few people share Alan's motive for leadership.

THE TWO MOTIVES

At the most fundamental level, there are only two motives that drive people to become a leader. First, they want to serve others, to do whatever is necessary to bring about something good for the people they lead. They understand that sacrifice and suffering are inevitable in this pursuit and that serving others is the only valid motivation for leadership. This is why it annoys me when people praise someone for being a "servant leader," as though there is any other valid option.

The second basic reason why people choose to be a leader—the all-too-common but invalid one—is that they want to be rewarded. They see leadership as the prize for years of hard work and are drawn by its trappings: attention, status, power, money. Most people understand intuitively that this is a terrible reason to become a leader, but it's important to identify specifically and tangibly why this is such a problem.

When leaders are motivated by personal reward, they will avoid the unpleasant situations and activities that leadership requires. They will calculate the personal economics of uncomfortable and tedious responsibilities—responsibilities that only a leader can do—and try to avoid them. This inevitably leaves the ✓ people in their charge without direction, guidance, and protection, which eventually hurts those people and the organization as a whole. Employees will express their disbelief as to how their leader could have been so negligent and irresponsible, yet it makes perfect sense in light of his or her motive for becoming a leader. An analogy might help us understand how this can prevent someone from being successful.

A father who maintains the belief that being a parent should be convenient and fun is going to have a hard time embracing the concept of spending a lot of time with his children or attending their activities. As long as he maintains the notion that dads shouldn't have to frequently sacrifice their own interests for the needs of their kids, then the most you can expect from him is begrudging compliance when it comes to an occasional game of Chutes and Ladders or a trip to Chuck E. Cheese, to mention nothing of changing dirty diapers or helping with algebra homework. Only by shifting the underlying attitude about what it means to be a parent can that dad become a good one.

When it comes to leading an organization, I've found that reward-centered leaders operate under a similar assumption: their role should be convenient and enjoyable. So they delegate, abdicate, or ignore situations that only the leader can address, leaving a painful and destructive vacuum. What makes this so problematic is that most of them don't even understand the flawed nature of their motive for leadership. Many even take pride in it!

Well, it's time to expose reward-centered leadership for what it is and help leaders overcome it, for their own good and the good of the people and organizations they are supposed to be serving. That is what this book is all about. In the following pages, I will first explore in detail the two different motives for leadership. Then I'll describe the dangerous omissions of reward-centered leaders, while helping them identify and adjust their own leadership motives.

EXPLORING THE TWO LEADERSHIP MOTIVES

Reward-centered leadership: the belief that being a leader is the reward for hard work; therefore, the experience of being a leader should be pleasant and enjoyable, free to choose what they work on and avoid anything mundane, unpleasant, or uncomfortable.

Responsibility-centered leadership: the belief that being a leader is a responsibility; therefore, the experience of leading should be difficult and challenging (though certainly not without elements of personal gratification).

No leader is purely reward-centered or responsibility-centered. We all struggle at times, and we all rise up to do the right thing at times. But one of these two motives for leadership will be predominant, and that motive will have a profound impact on the success of the leader and the organization he or she serves.

To make this a little easier to understand, let's use another analogy.

Imagine young men being drafted into the National Football League. When some players get chosen by a team, they feel primarily a great sense of relief and accomplishment. "I've finally made it. After years of hard work, I'm being rewarded and recognized. My life is about to become more enjoyable, and I don't have to worry about money. I can't wait to celebrate, find a house, buy a car, …"

Other players, though grateful for and gratified by their accomplishment, immediately feel the weight of proving their worth to the team that drafted them. "I can't wait to get my new playbook and start preparing for the season. I don't want my coaches and teammates to look back on this next year and regret choosing me. I need to find a place to live as soon as possible and get to work improving on…"

There is a fundamental difference between these players, one that will almost always have a greater impact on their eventual success than their talents and skills. Simply stated, players who are responsibility-centered almost always exceed expectations. Players who are reward-centered almost always fail to live up to theirs.

Though this may seem obvious, it's worth asking these "how" questions. How does a leader's motive play out in the organization? How does it impact the day-to-day activities of his or her work? The answers have everything to do with behavior. To illustrate this, let's go back to the football player analogy and assume that the players are wide receivers. (My apologies to readers who don't know anything about football. Wide receivers are the players who catch passes thrown to them by the quarterback.)

Here is what the reward-centered receiver is *not* going to do. He *won't* work out as much in the off-season as the responsibility-centered receiver. He *won't* block as hard during games when he's not getting the ball thrown to him. And he probably *won't* extend himself as much to catch a difficult pass across the middle of the field if he thinks he might get hit hard. He will get out-worked, out-blocked, and out-hustled.

Or imagine two candidates for president of a country. One focuses on getting elected and sees that day as the crowning achievement of his or her life. The other sees the election as the beginning of his or her attempt to accomplish something great. Should it be at all surprising that, all other things being equal, the second will be a much better president than the first? But again, it's worth asking the question, what behaviors is the reward-centered president going to avoid? Here are a few: taking the time to understand important legislative issues, meeting with constituents who offer little opportunity for publicity, adhering to traditions that are personally uninteresting to him or her. The other candidate is going to embrace those responsibilities.

The same applies to leaders of organizations, and I've seen this again and again during the twenty-plus years I've been consulting to CEOs and their teams, even if I didn't understand it completely at the time.

I've seen all too many extremely talented CEOs squander their opportunities to lead their organizations because they saw their job as a playground for their curiosities and predilections. I've seen them ignore real problems that didn't excite them and walk away from situations that held no promise of glory or noto-riety or fun. And I will admit that in my own moments of reward-centered leadership, I've seen myself avoid these things too. It's not pretty, and it has a real impact on the organizations and people we lead.

On the other hand, I've also seen relatively ordi-nary people lead their organizations to greater heights than anyone expected because they believed it was their responsibility to do the most mundane and uncomfortable jobs and tasks. They knew that giving speeches and being in the spotlight was a very small part of their work and that the daily grind of keeping the organization moving in the right direction was their real job.

Again, none of us are perfect leaders. We all find ourselves tempted—and sometimes we give in to the temptation—to be reward-centered, to seek out opportunities that we find fun, and to ignore anything that is tedious or unpleasant. But over time, those who choose to embrace responsibility-centered leadership—even if they were formerly focused on rewards—will come to see activities and situations that they once viewed as tedious and unpleasant as the real work of a selfless leader. And they'll eventually start to enjoy them.

Now let's take a look at the situations and activities that reward-centered leaders tend to delegate, abdicate, or ignore.

THE FIVE OMISSIONS
OF REWARD-CENTERED
LEADERS

hat follows are the five situations or responsibilities that reward-centered leaders delegate, abdicate, or avoid altogether, which cause the greatest problems for the people they lead. The omission of one or all of these areas may be an indication of an improper motive for leading.

Let me make it clear that this is not a list of the primary responsibilities of a leader. That is a different kind of list. and something I address more thoroughly in my book *The Advantage*. These are simply the most common omissions that reward-centered leaders find to be tedious, uncomfortable, or just plain hard. At the end of each section are a few questions to help you reflect on your own attitude and discern whether you may be struggling to some extent with reward-centered leadership.

1. DEVELOPING THE LEADERSHIP TEAM

Just about every leader will give lip service to the importance of building his or her executive team. This is why it is so surprising that this activity is often delegated, and sometimes even abdicated completely, by many CEOs and other organizational leaders.

In some cases, leaders delegate team-building to their head of HR. Let me be very clear; this does not work. And that's not a knock against HR folks. If people on a leadership team don't believe that the leader sees team development as one of his or her most critical roles, they're not going to take it seriously, and it's not going to be effective. The leader simply must take personal responsibility for, and participate actively in, the task of building his or her team.

There are a few reasons why intelligent executives would allow someone else to assume responsibility for building their team. First, they don't see it as being central to the success of the organization. In spite of what they might claim publicly, too many leaders still believe teamwork is a soft pursuit, less important than more technical matters like finance or strategy or marketing. So they choose to stay involved in those technical areas and let someone else handle the soft stuff.

Second, leaders often realize that effective team-building always involves emotional and uncomfortable conversations. Few leaders, even the good ones, look forward to those awkward moments and prefer to let others deal with them. They sit back and hope that a colleague or internal consultant will manage the emotions, allowing them to get the benefits of building a team without the messy cost. This never works.

In some cases, leaders don't delegate the building of a team to HR; they simply ignore it altogether. They often excuse this by dismissing team-building as something touchy-feely and irrelevant to the bottom line. Now, I'll be the first to agree with their distaste for wasting time on irrelevant experiential exercises involving climbing trees or building human pyramids. But I'll disagree with them much more fervently for failing to see teamwork as the practical, tangible competitive advantage that it is, one that actually enables the success of marketing, finance, strategy, and all of those other more technical pursuits.

Leader Reflection and Call to Action

This would be a good time to step back and ask yourself a couple of questions about your willingness to focus on developing your team.

- Do you feel that spending time developing your team members' interpersonal dynamics is superfluous or a waste of time?

- Do you organize "team-building" activities for your team that are fun but that largely ignore uncomfortable conversations about their collective behaviors?

If you answered *yes* to these questions, you may have the wrong motive for leading, and you have a serious decision to make. You can either rethink your attitude about team-building and embrace it as the practical, indispensable discipline that it is, or you can accept that the organization you lead will never come close to reaching its full potential and that your team members will suffer unnecessarily. I promise that I'm not being overly dramatic here. Those really are the stakes.

2. MANAGING SUBORDINATES (AND MAKING THEM MANAGE THEIRS)

When it comes to managing executives as individuals (as opposed to dealing with them collectively as a team), many of the leaders I've worked with over the years struggle, especially those closer to the top of organizations. This is the result of a few things.

On the one hand, many of them have been trained to see management as a set of bureaucratic, overly structured activities related to writing detailed objectives, conducting performance reviews, and determining compensation. This is not really management, either at the executive level or the front line. Managing individuals is about helping them set the general direction of their work, ensuring that it is aligned with and understood by their peers, and staying informed enough to identify potential obstacles and problems as early as possible. It is also about coaching leaders to improve themselves behaviorally to make it more likely that they will succeed.

I have found that CEOs often have far too little understanding of what their executives are working on, and they justify this by declaring that they "abhor micromanagement" or by claiming that they implicitly trust their subordinates. Of course, trusting someone is not an excuse for not managing them. And helping subordinates establish a direction and knowing how they are progressing is far from micro-management.

There is a secondary aspect of managing individuals that a leader must fulfill: they must ensure that their subordinates one level below are managing their people too! This is one of the most overlooked responsibilities that I find among senior leaders, especially CEOs. Even many CEOs who are really good people managers don't demand (e.g., check up on, remind and remind again) that their executives do the same for their employees.

All of this raises this question: how can really intelligent and hard-working leaders overlook something so basic and important as managing their subordinates? The simple fact of the matter is that many of them don't really *want* to have to manage them. Remember, reward-focused leaders are motivated by the idea that they can now pick and choose what to do based on what they like doing. They're motto might well be "It's good to be the king." And few "kings" want to be managers.

It's worth repeating that many of the reward-focused CEOs I've known will attempt to justify their abdication of managing their people by saying, "I hire experienced executives and I trust them. They shouldn't need me to manage them." Of course, this is inane. Managing someone is not a punitive activity, nor a sign of distrust. And it doesn't change based on a person's seniority or tenure. Management is the act of aligning people's actions, behaviors, and attitudes with the needs of the organization and making sure that little problems don't become big ones. Avoiding this is nothing but negligence.

Leader Reflection and Call to Action

Here are the questions that you should ask yourself about your willingness to actively manage your direct reports.

- Do you believe that providing individual guidance and coaching to your people is somehow beneath you or not worth your time?
- Do you feel that you should be able to trust them to manage themselves?
- Do you justify not knowing what your direct reports are doing by claiming not to want to be a micromanager?

If you answered *yes* to these questions, then your motive for leading may be off. You can either rethink your role and get more involved in coaching them around their work, or accept that they will often fail to meet your expectations and become misaligned with the goals of the team. It really is up to you.

 ### 3. HAVING DIFFICULT AND UNCOMFORTABLE CONVERSATIONS

While having difficult conversations is certainly one part of managing a team and subordinates, it has more to do with addressing uncomfortable behavioral issues in an organization. And because so many leaders try to avoid interpersonal discomfort, it needs to be treated separately.

One of the main responsibilities of a leader is to confront difficult, awkward issues quickly and with clarity, charity, and resolve. What kind of issues am I talking about? Everything from a team member's annoying mannerisms to poisonous interpersonal dynamics and politics. There isn't a leader out there who hasn't balked at a moment when they should have "entered the danger" and had a difficult conversation about these things. This makes sense, because I know that almost no chief executive likes to do this. Most loathe it. And yet, when leaders dodge these situations, they jeopardize the success of the team and the organization as a whole.

But don't get me wrong; I understand why leaders avoid these things. I've been there many times myself, and I've balked a few more times than I'd like to admit. But actually justifying the cowardice of avoiding difficult conversations by claiming not to have time or energy or interest is absurd, because it is built upon the ridiculous notion that the ignored issue won't eventually degrade the organization's performance.

Though I'm sure there are more out there, I've met only one leader who actually seemed to enjoy the idea of confronting his people. And he would address just about anything, from not being prepared for presentations to looking at their phones during meetings to being rude to their colleagues. He is Alan Mulally, whom I mentioned before.

One of the keys to Alan's success was something I call "joyful accountability." He liked to approach people who needed correction and cheerfully let them know that it was completely up to them whether they changed their behavior or attitude. He would remind them that if they couldn't change, he would still be their friend, but they couldn't continue to work at Ford, or Boeing.

Alan was neither passive-aggressive nor condescending when he said these things. He meant every word. And more often than not, people he confronted changed their behavior. Plenty of times, they chose to leave the organization, which is a heck of a lot better than them staying and continuing their behavior and having to go through a lengthy, painful, and expensive process of being let go. And for those who left, it was better, and more dignified, that they chose to leave of their own volition.

Wouldn't it be naïve, if not disingenuous, to deny that Alan's success at Boeing and Ford had something to do with his willingness to have difficult, uncomfortable conversations with his people? I certainly think so. So does he. He knew that building or turning around an organization started with changing the behaviors of the leaders who worked for him, which led to behavioral change in the rest of the organization.

And this is true for any leader. Failing to confront people quickly about small issues is a guarantee that they will become big issues. And if you're not a responsibility-centered leader, one who understands that if the leader doesn't do it, no one will, then you're probably going to find a reason, almost any reason, to ignore those messy issues and do something else.

Before moving on from this topic, it's probably worth taking a moment to call out the simple underlying reason that most people avoid difficult conversations: it is embarrassing and awkward. There is nothing comfortable about turning to a man or woman whom you know, someone who is of similar age to you, and who is talented in their own right, and telling them something that makes them feel momentarily bad.

I have to admit that I don't like doing this, and I used to be really, really hesitant to do it. Until one day I realized that holding back and avoiding those conversations was actually <u>an act of selfishness</u>. I wasn't avoiding those conversations for the sake of my employees' feelings, but for my own! In the end, I was trading off my discomfort for theirs, leaving them to experience even greater pain when their shortcomings manifested themselves during a performance review, a compensation discussion, or worse yet, an exit interview. Ouch. And that's to say nothing of what it did to the organization as a whole.

Examples

What follows are a few real-world anecdotes of leaders who didn't understand the benefits of engaging in uncomfortable conversations.

- *I once attended a client's leadership team meeting and watched in disbelief as a disrespectful and irritating executive fell asleep for a long period of time, right in front of the CEO. She said nothing to him, even after the meeting was over.*
- *I knew the chief information officer of a large and well-known company. I'll call him Fred. One day Fred learned, via a company-wide e-mail announcement, that the CEO whom he worked for had hired a new CIO. Since the CEO never bothered*

to tell him that he was being replaced, Fred called his office to schedule a meeting. The CEO's assistant said she could find no time for them to meet, and the CEO avoided seeing Fred for weeks. At one point the two men were sitting across from one another on the company's private plane, and the CEO pretended to be asleep to avoid a conversation. Eventually, Fred just left the company on his own. (I promise I'm not making that up. And believe it or not, that CEO went on to write a book on leadership.)

- *A friend of mine was an HR generalist at a sizeable company, supporting an executive within human resources. One day the human resources executive called her into his office. He explained to her that one of his employees had body odor, and he wanted her to confront the smelly employee because he didn't want to do it himself.*

- *The CEO of a company was in the midst of a search for a new chief operating officer. An unpopular member of his executive team (Fred) began telling his peers that he was going to get the job, which would make him their boss. The concerned executives did not relish the idea of working for Fred, and so they confronted the CEO about the situation. He assured them it wasn't true, but when they encouraged him to confront and correct Fred, the executive explained that he "didn't have the time or energy for that kind of stuff."*

Leader Reflection and Call to Action

Ask yourself the following questions about your willingness to have difficult and uncomfortable conversations.

- Would you rather learn to live with a person's difficult behaviors than endure an awkward, potentially emotional discussion with them?
- Do you find yourself venting about your direct reports' behavioral issues rather than talking with them directly?

If you answered *yes* to these questions, this may be an indication that your leadership motive needs to be adjusted. You will need to reset your expectations about how "comfortable" your job is supposed to be and find the courage to start entering into dangerous conversations until it becomes natural. Or you should prepare for increasing levels of politics, morale problems, and unwanted turnover on your team and in your organization.

4. RUNNING GREAT TEAM MEETINGS

Meetings remain one of the most unpopular and underestimated activities in business. It is where leaders make decisions about whether to purchase a competitor or sell itself to one, to hire more employees or lay them off, to implement a new strategy or kill an old one. Can there be a more critical, central, or indispensable activity within an organization than a meeting?

I won't go into great detail here about the specific activities involved in running an effective meeting, because that is the subject of an entirely different and longer book. In the context of this book, I'll simply focus on the shocking reality that in so many organizations the people responsible for making meetings better—more effective and less boring—often complain about them the most!

So many CEOs and other leaders of organizations aren't afraid to admit that they dread meetings, which they see as a sort of penance. And so they simply tolerate and "get through" awful meetings, rather than making them as focused, relevant, and intense as they should be. Some even try to avoid them altogether.

Let's step back from all this and put it into perspective. A leader seeing his or her meetings as drudgery would be like a doctor viewing surgery that way. Or a teacher thinking about class lectures that way. Or a quarterback seeing games that way. As I said earlier, meetings are the setting, the arena, the moment when the most important discussions and decisions take place. What could be more important?

Think about it this way. The best place to observe whether a surgeon is good at her job, a teacher is good at his, or a quarterback is good at his, is to watch them during an operation, a class session, or a game, respectively. What is the best place to observe a leader? That's right—a meeting.

When leaders accept the less-than-amazing status of meetings, the results are two-fold. First, and most important of all, it leads to bad decision-making. The fact is, if meetings are not engaging, it's completely logical to conclude that the quality of those decisions will be subpar. I cannot fathom—or for that matter, measure—how to adequately gauge the impact this has on the performance and success of an organization. But it is undoubtedly enormous.

The second problem of accepting bad meetings at the executive level is that it sets the precedent for the rest of the organization. <u>What is tolerated at the top of a company is often the ceiling of what can be expected deeper within it.</u> That's not to say that some managers won't try, on their own, to make their meetings more effective than those of their boss. But it's unlikely that they'll feel much pressure to do so. Contrast that with a manager whose CEO runs fantastic meetings. He or she is likely to want his or her meetings to measure up to those standards. <u>This is not rocket science.</u>

Examples

What follows are a few real-world anecdotes of leaders who didn't embrace the critical nature of meetings.

- *I once worked with a very charismatic CEO who hated meetings. He would frequently "check out" during conversations, looking down at the chair next to him where he had laid out the sports page. What was so amazing about this was that everyone on his team knew he was doing it, but they seemed to have resigned themselves to the fact that he just wasn't going to be interested in detailed conversations about the business unless those conversations held some personal interest for him. His company eventually imploded in a way that surprised everyone, and the CEO's disconnect and disinterest in business fundamentals was a big part of that implosion.*

- *Another CEO I knew found meetings to be largely a tactical, administrative exercise. He wasn't going to cancel them but simply wanted to reduce his own investment in them. So he delegated the design and facilitation of executive staff meetings to his head of HR. Members of the executive team, including the HR VP, found those meetings to be dispassionate, and attributed it to the CEO's lack of interest in what was going on.*

Leader Reflection and Call to Action

Here are the questions that you should ask yourself about your meetings.

- Do you complain about your own meetings being boring or ineffective, and do you long for the end of them?
- Do you allow your people, and yourself, to check out during those meetings, or perhaps skip them from time to time for "more important" work?

If you answered *yes* to these questions, you may have a problem with your leadership motive. You can pour yourself into designing and facilitating more intense, focused meetings. Or you can resign yourself to suboptimal decision-making, reduced innovation, and a good deal of regret. Easy choice, right?

5. COMMUNICATING CONSTANTLY AND REPETITIVELY TO EMPLOYEES

Most CEOs don't hate the idea of communicating to employees. But the majority of them greatly under-estimate the amount of communication that is necessary. As a result, they think they've done an adequate job announcing a new strategy or initiative long before most people, even many senior-level employees, are close to understanding and embracing it. Recently I met with a CEO and his head of HR. The CEO said, "We have to save this company." The head of HR said, "I've never heard you say that before." The CEO said, "I thought I'd been saying it for the past year." Do you think that employees in the organization are hearing and internalizing that message if one of the executives isn't?

I've read studies that say employees have to hear a message seven times before they believe executives are serious about it. Until then, they discount it as corporate speak or internal propaganda. Though it's been a while since I was a line-level employee, I can remember taking most corporate communication from executives with a grain of salt. That is unless they reinforced it so much over time that I overcame my skepticism.

Unfortunately, many CEOs refuse to repeat themselves again and again and again and again. There are a few reasons for this. Many of them worry that they're going to insult their audience by repeating a message. They forget that employees hate not knowing what's going on in their organization and that no reasonable human being has ever left a company because management communicated too much. "That's it. I'm going somewhere where leaders tell me something once and never repeat it again!" Though it is always much better to err on the side of excessive communication, most leaders are far more comfortable on the other end of the risk profile.

Another reason that CEOs, especially the reward-centered ones, fail to communicate enough is that they get bored with their messages. "Haven't we done this presentation about our core purpose and values enough? What else do we have?" They fail to appreciate that the purpose of communication is not their own entertainment. Nor is it simply the dissemination of information. The reason a CEO communicates to employees, at all levels, is to ensure that people are aligned with and have bought into what is going on and where they fit into the success of the enterprise. It is an emotional and behavioral process more than a transactional and informational one. And it requires real, repetitive, sometimes tedious work from a leader.

The very best leaders in the corporate world understand this and don't hesitate to repeat themselves. They see themselves as CROs—chief reminding officers. Whether they're giving a talk at an employee event, sending out an e-mail reminder to employees, telling the story of the company's founding during orientation, writing a letter in an internal newsletter, or having lunch with employees in a far-flung office, they stick to the most fundamental messages, knowing that employees need to hear those messages again and again and again and ... you get it. Of course, good leaders try to be creative when they reinforce messages. But they are far more concerned about employees being uninformed than they are about being criticized for redundancy.

Examples

What follows are a few real-world anecdotes of leaders who understand the importance of over-communication.

- *One CEO I knew had always believed in being a CRO. He was constantly reminding employees, every opportunity he could find, about the fundamentals of the organization and the importance of customers. And then he began getting pushback—from the people on his own executive team! "I think you need to get some new material," they would tease him, only partially in jest. He was on the verge of giving in to their exhortations until he read one of my books, where I introduce the concept of the chief reminding officer. "See," he told them, "I'm supposed to do this!" He convinced them that even though they might have heard his messages enough, employees in the organization needed to be reminded even more.*

- *Perhaps the best chief reminding officer I've known is Gary Kelly, the long-time CEO of Southwest Airlines. I've seen him speak to executives as well as employees many times over the course of a decade and more. I've also been reading his monthly letter to employees and customers in the company's in-flight magazine. Again and again and again, Gary addresses the same topics at the heart of Southwest's culture and strategy. He finds different ways to do it so that it's interesting and new, but he doesn't stray from the messages that he is responsible for keeping alive.*

- *The other world-class CRO I know is, yes, Alan Mullaly. When he took over Ford, he put together a simple but effective plan for turning around the company. The* Wall Street Journal *invited him for an interview, and he presented that plan to them for an article. A year later, the* Journal *invited him back for an update, and Alan proceeded to share the plan with them again. They asked him for something new, as they had already covered that content. Alan simply explained that the plan was the plan, and his job was to keep his company focused on it, not to move from one flavor of the month to another.*

Leader Reflection and Call to Action

Ask yourself the following questions about your willingness to communicate constantly and repetitively.

- Do you resent having to repeat yourself, complaining that your employees don't listen?
- Do you look for new messages and ideas to communicate because you get bored saying the same things again and again?

If you answered *yes* to these questions, your motive for leadership may not be quite right. You need to change your general attitude about communication and see it as a tool for helping others understand and internalize important ideas rather than an activity for your own entertainment. Otherwise, you'll need to come to terms with the fact that your employees, even your executives, will often be confused and misaligned. And you'll need to get used to being surprised and frustrated by their inability to understand you and get on board with your plans.

SUMMARY

Again, these five areas—building a leadership team, managing subordinates, having difficult conversations, running effective meetings, and constantly repeating key messages to employees—are *not* a list of the key responsibilities of the leader of an organization. These are simply the situations and responsibilities that leaders avoid all too often when they don't see it as their job to do the things that no one else can.

IMPERFECTION AND VIGILANCE

Because no one is perfect, no leader has a pure leadership motive. All of us are tempted to be reward-centered at times, and the vast majority will occasionally give in to that temptation. However, one of the two motives eventually will become dominant in the day-to-day work of leading. And that is why it's important for any leader to understand his or her predominant motive and do whatever it takes to move closer and closer to the purely responsibility-centered one.

It's important to understand that even those who seem to master responsibility-centered leadership are not immune from slipping. Because we human beings are fallible, and prone to flattery and fatigue, even the best of us can slide almost unconsciously into reward-centered leadership.

This happens because responsibility-centered leaders will inevitably receive praise for their humility and selflessness, even though they are merely doing what they ought to do as leaders. With this praise, it becomes almost natural for them to start comparing themselves to reward-centered leaders, and gradually lower their standards. One day a leader can wake up and realize that he or she is avoiding situations and responsibilities that seem thankless.

On a final and related note, it is critical that responsibility-centered leaders—and even those who aren't—confront the reality that the people they lead are probably not telling them the unvarnished truth about their behavior. For every morsel of constructive feedback a leader gets, there will be a dozen compliments, many of them unwarranted. And even when this is understood in theory, it is very, very difficult for any leader, even the most humble of them, to avoid letting constant approval and admiration create a warped and inaccurate self-image. This is why it is so important for leaders to surround themselves with people who will be honest with them.

THE SURPRISING DANGER OF FUN

I t's worth noting that not all reward-centered leaders look alike, nor are they seeking the same rewards. For instance, some leaders seek attention and status as their reward; this is probably the most common kind. Others may be more motivated by power.

However, many reward-centered leaders are not overtly motivated by those pride-related incentives, but rather by their desire to spend their time doing what they find to be enjoyable, entertaining, or fun. Yes, fun. As innocent as this may seem, it is particularly dangerous because, well, because it seems harmless.

Fun-centered leaders can easily justify their behavior or minimize the harm it causes because, after all, they're not as ego-driven as others who want attention and status. But the vacuum created by leaders who avoid important activities simply because they don't find them enjoyable or entertaining is no less problematic. And at the end of the day, even leaders who seek fun are doing so for themselves. Trust me. I've made this mistake myself

THE END OF SERVANT LEADERSHIP

The Motive is the shortest and simplest book I've written to date, but I suspect that it may be the most important. That's because the danger of leading for the wrong reason is so high, not only for individuals, but for society as a whole.

I fear that too many people have come to tolerate, even expect, leaders to be self-centered. Too many employees are resigned to executives in their company who take action only when it is in their own interests. Too many executives are resigned to working for CEOs who can't be expected to do the things they find uncomfortable or uninteresting. And too many citizens are resigned to civic leaders who make decisions about policy based on their poll numbers and their ability to get elected or be popular.

And so, if reward-centered, self-centered leadership becomes the norm, young people will grow up believing that this is what it means to be a leader. The wrong people will aspire to be managers, CEOs, and civic leaders, condemning society to more of the same for generations to come. This can't be allowed to happen.

I believe it's long past time that we, as individuals and as a society, reestablished the standard that leadership can never be about the leader more than the led. Employees need to point out reward-centered leadership when they see it in their managers. Executives need to commit to changing it when they realize it is true about themselves. And citizens need to speak out against it when they see it in their appointed and elected civil servants.

If we can restore the collective attitude that leadership is meant to be a joyfully difficult and selfless responsibility, I am convinced that we will see companies become more successful, employees more engaged and fulfilled, and society more optimistic and hopeful. Perhaps people will stop using the term "servant leadership" altogether, because everyone will understand that it is the only valid kind. And that is certainly worth doing.

ACKNOWLEDGMENTS

After 11 books, acknowledgments feel a bit rote, but they are no less important and sincere. My wife, Laura, and my boys, Matthew, Connor, Casey, and Michael, have more and more influence on my work than ever, and your support and love are gifts beyond measure.

My team at The Table Group is like a second family, providing me with encouragement, ideas, and accountability, without which I could never write any books at all. And special gratitude, as always, to Tracy for your amazingly insightful ideas and edits throughout the process, on matters large and small.

Thanks to everyone at Wiley for the support and freedom you give us. I can't believe that after 20 years, we still find ways to work better together. And thanks to my agent, Jim Levine, for your constant guidance and sincere interest in all we do.

Of course, my gratitude for everything, including the people above, is for my Lord and Savior, Jesus. Without You, I can do nothing.

ABOUT THE AUTHOR

Patrick Lencioni is founder and president of The Table Group, a firm dedicated to helping leaders improve their organizations' health since 1997. His principles have been embraced by leaders around the world and adopted by organizations of virtually every kind, including multinational corporations, entrepreneurial ventures, professional sports teams, the military, non-profits, schools, and churches.

Lencioni is the author of eleven business books with nearly seven million copies sold worldwide. His work has appeared in the *Wall Street Journal, Harvard Business Review, Fortune, Bloomberg Business-week*, and *USA Today*, among other publications.

Prior to founding The Table Group, Lencioni served as an executive at Sybase, Inc. He started his career at Bain & Company and later worked at Oracle Corporation.

Lencioni lives in the San Francisco Bay Area with his wife and their four sons.

To learn more about Patrick and The Table Group, please visit www.tablegroup.com.

tablegroup

Patrick Lencioni is founder of The Table Group, a firm dedicated to changing the world of work. The Table Group provides executives, team leaders, managers and employees with everything they need to make their organizations healthier, teams more cohesive, and people more engaged and fulfilled.

www.**Table**Group.com

VISIT OUR
WEBSITE & EXPLORE:

CONSULTING

SPEAKING

BOOKS

PRODUCTS

FREE RESOURCES

PODCAST